THE LOUSIER WAR

The Lousier War

W. A. TUCKER

NEW ENGLISH LIBRARY
TIMES MIRROR

To
Dorothy, my wife,
and
Cynthia, our daughter.

An NEL Original
© W. A. Tucker, 1974

*

FIRST NEL PAPERBACK EDITION JULY 1974

This new edition September 1975

*

NEL Books are published by The New English Library Limited from Barnard's Inn, Holborn, London E.C.1. Made and printed in Great Britain by C. Nicholls & Company Ltd

4500 2635 3

THE LOUSIER WAR

*

the story of a
wartime volunteer
in

Kitchener's Army
1914–1918

who was
taken prisoner
by the Germans
after serving on the
Western Front and Italy

*

A FACTUAL NARRATIVE

I wrote this narrative only after considerable persuasion from friends who thought that my World War I experiences merited compilation in readable form.

"Who now wants to read about the first World War anyway?" I argued many times.

"We do," came the resounding answer on just as many occasions; and the younger people seemed the more insistent on that point.

I suppose some of the vicissitudes that came my way, particularly when I was a prisoner in German hands, were unusual. Indeed the British Imperial War Museum requested the typescript of these Memoirs for its archives because, the curator explained, they were very short of such accounts of life in German prisoner concentrations in the 1914–18 war.

On reflection, there were many aspects of the first World War, terrible and not so terrible, that have not recurred and are never likely to. It is therefore not surprising that those born so long after should find of absorbing interest the tales of those who actually went through it.

There were certainly some excellent contemporary accounts of the actual battles and life in the trenches but, with a few notable exceptions, they were very chauvinistic and one-sided. The several graphic publications of the period, while well produced, naturally mirrored the popular feeling of hate and contempt for the enemy so efficiently worked up by the Allied propagandists. Dramatic pictures of battles always portrayed British soldiers of magnificient stature, impeccably uniformed and equipped, often with forehead heavily bandaged but gallantly fighting on regardless; while their luckless German adversaries were either lying killed in droves or cringing in unsoldierly disarray in face of British bayonets.

While the going is good, therefore, it might after all serve a purpose if one of the survivors tells his story with the advantage of the balanced look-back that an interval of 50 years or more offers. The present average age of those in the British Army of 1914 must be about 80 years, so before long, relatively speaking, there will be no survivors of those bloody four years.

In my opinion the most predominant feature of this lengthy hindsight is that the German soldier was no Unspeakable Hun. And we now know that the Kaiser did not refer to the British Expeditionary Force as "contemptible"; and our people could have been spared the horror of believing that the invading Germans held Belgian babies aloft on their bayonets. These are but two out of shoals of lies. When we consider how deep has seeped the connotation "Contemptible" (survivors of the Mons Retreat are almost officially known as The Old Contemptibles) it is incredible that the fable has been allowed to kid us for more than 50 years.

British propaganda was far more clever than the German effort. They had stunts like their stolid Hymn of Hate and Gott Strafe England but what were they compared with What did You do in the Great War, Daddy?; We don't want to lose You, But we think You ought to Go; and The Angels of Mons? Lord Northcliffe, one time Director of Propaganda, wrote that propaganda should be "the pace-maker for policy and should form Opinion without Opinion realizing that it is being formed". What an ornamental way of saying that the public should be tricked! Or more bluntly the technique of putting lies in such a way that they will appear facts.

As a prisoner for the closing nine months of the war I had contact with the German soldiers in the war area, more by far than the ordinary prisoner. Had the private troopers exchanged uniforms with the British I could have proved very little difference in their reactions, and in my stories I have tried hard to be fair and truthful about it.

The German machine, however, operated from Command, was a different matter and most of the inhumanities found their source therefrom. For our part we prisoners were no angels. Wars are not love affairs and we therefore did all we could to obstruct the enemy's war effort, whether as prisoners or combatants.

Although I repeat my opinion that even in those days there were many indistinguishable Anglo-German characteristics there *were* some – and they remain so – that are as different as chalk and cheese. One was, and still is, the greater German respect (or fear) for discipline and authority. The British are not psychologically conditioned to the same extent.

Stand today at any town traffic lights in Germany: though

there is not even a wheel-barrow in sight, you will not see a German attempt to cross the road before the light goes full green. But watch a traffic intersection in, say, London's Oxford Street. If there is no traffic within 100 ft will you see anyone wait until the light turns green?

This kind of obedience caused the Germans to administer to the letter all those privations inflicted on prisoners which I will describe.

An adjustment that I have seen over sixty or so years is in the relative living standard, cultural and material, between the United Kingdom and our Continental neighbours, and this I assert was responsible for the somewhat rougher treatment applied by the Germans when they had the opportunity. The history of mankind is that not only different human species have their turn at the top of the cultural and civilized cycle but also nations – Persia, Egypt, Greece, Rome, for example. Many will say that some of the European belligerents in the 1914–18 war have now overhauled us, notably Western Germany. But when the British Expeditionary Force first arrived in France, the sanitation, plumbing, housing and social arrangements struck the British Tommy as extremely crude. And when the British Army of Occupation reached Western Germany at the end of 1918 they found many aspects of life there below their own standards at home. (As late as 1954 toilet paper was meted out by a female attendant in rations of three strips to travellers using the lavatory at Cologne's main railway station.)

I have often been asked how far religious faith entered the minds of those combatant Tommies who were never far from being killed. To outward appearances, very little. Whereas the great majority promptly replied C. of E. to the recruiting officer's inquiry as to their religion, worshippers who could be called devout were extremely rare. A few Roman Catholics I knew would go to extraordinary lengths to attend Mass whenever possible; they always seemed uplifted by these occasions and were held in great respect by the other men for their evident sincerity. As for the others it required compulsory parades to ensure a satisfactory attendance and these, it must be recorded, were unpopular with the men in the war areas because, after a spell in the trenches, they would rather have rested. Nevertheless, I never heard a single soldier declare himself an Unbeliever. On the other hand I never heard any prayers for deliverance from the most perilous of plights, yet, in the circumstances, I am sure many prayed in silence.

Generally, the old soldiers will pay tribute to the Church

Army. This organization under the control of army chaplains placed its portable wooden huts immediately behind the fighting lines. From these the men could get hot drinks and cigarettes, play games like ping pong, write letters and rest near warm stoves.

Did it often happen that our men broke down under bombardments, desert, or show cowardice? No it didn't. I never saw a British soldier quit in any circumstances, but as men were shot for it we all supposed it did happen. Anyway, in three years up front I personally never saw a single instance, and considering the British *combatant* strength in France averaged 1,200,000 men the proportion who couldn't take it was negligible. I have seen men pale with fright – I have been that way myself - but I never saw a man run the other way.

Surveying the changes in our attitude to authority compared with the 1914–18 era, many of us have come to the conclusion that the army discipline we had to tolerate was not a bad thing after all. Much as we young soldiers cursed it at the time, it instilled in us a respect for order. Maybe the war canalized the violence which seems to be instinctive in man but that same fury was controlled; by command it was turned off and on, like a tap. Whether that is better or worse than the widespread but haphazard violence of today will be argued by the moralists.

To conclude this foreword, surely no one can drive along the roads of Northern France and Belgium through the forests of 1914–18 grave-stones and remain unmoved by the very obvious disregard for young lives in that war. The British left 851,117 dead there plus 142,057 missing. With wounded the total was nearly 3,000,000. The German casualties were said to be twice as many.

The lunacy of it was further accentuated by the fact that the two main antagonists are alike in racial characteristics and both second to none in the universe for those material, scientific, technological and cultural attainments which are regarded as the best aspects of human progress. If the British and the Germans had united their achievements instead of committing fratricide, their combination would have put a very different slant on who is a so-called Super Power today.

I

WELCOME TO THE FORCES (1914 style)

"And what the hell do *you* want here?" barked the sergeant in charge of the improvised Recruiting Depot.

He was a formidable example of the traditional Bully Sergeant, beetle-browed and moustached.

Chilled, but dogged, I replied, "I've come to join your Battalion." I pulled what I imagined might be the kind of face that would make my 17 years of age look like 19 at least.

"Oh you have, have you!" observed the sergeant. "Well you can sling yer bloody hook and run home to mother" he roared. "You haven't got the cradle marks off your arse yet. And we want no shortarse rookies in this lot either," he added.

This was the kind of reception that greeted countless British youths after they had queued for hours outside recruiting centres in the hope of being accepted for the fighting line in the days following the outbreak of war in 1914.

The immediate reaction by Britons all over the world was surely a phenomenon which could happen only once. We shall never know, because the eventual disintegration of the British Empire dissolves any prospect of its recurrence even if modern youth held the same jingoistic reverence for the Union Jack.

Making every allowance for the patriotic, flag-wagging fervour which agitates most nationals of any country when war looks likely, there must have been something extraordinary about the British reaction. That millions of men, thousands from all corners of the globe, should be *volunteering* to fight was something that most other countries just did not understand. For example, when I was eventually a prisoner in German hands the German soldiers were fond of asking —

"Tommy; du freiwilliger?" (Did you volunteer?) When the answer was Yes, the German soldier would almost always tap his head to imply I was a lunatic.

In fact volunteers for the British Army supplied all the man power they could cope with for nearly 18 months; compulsory service did not effectively take shape until well into 1916.

11

And so I became one of the many thousands of under-aged (and under-developed youths who spent every day for many weeks after August 4, 1914 submitting to military medical inspections and caustic comments in vain endeavour to "take the King's shilling" (as actual enlistment was then colloquially called): until one day late in August 1914 when I wriggled into the ranks of a London Territorial Army Unit known as the 10th County of London Battalion.

Being only 17 years old I had to swear on oath that I was 19, the lowest age of acceptance by the military for the real stuff. I turned up daily for parades at Battalion Headquarters at Hackney in East London — but only for one week. On parade one morning at the end of exactly seven days of "soldiering", I was aware of a corporal yelling "You, you, you and *you*. Line up and stand at attention!".

I gradually became fearfully aware that I was the *you*. The Colonel of the Battalion was now alarmingly near and he proceeded to take a closer look at the four of us.

The Colonel looked contemptuously down at quivering me. I did all I could to assume the stance and demeanour of a hard-boiled warrior; After a few glances of marked disapproval, our worthy Colonel simply said —

"You. Two paces forward" I stepped out of the line.

"Now then" he added. "What is your *real* age?"

"Nineteen, sir" I answered.

"Really. Does your mother know? Report at once to the Battalion doctor."

The doctor simply ignored my bleatings that I had passed all medical tests only the previous week.

"Yes my boy" said the doctor. "Your heart is not too good". He casually placed his hand over my clothed chest.

"You are discharged," he added.

It seemed this was the favourite way in those days of getting rid of recruits who were both under the age and under-brawned. Many thousands of boys, well under 19 years of age, did get through, provided they had the physical bulk and stature that went with a traditional soldier. The regular officers resented having obvious kids under their command on parades which were often under public gaze.

II

A WELSHMAN BY ENLISTMENT

During the next two months my several attempts to re-enter
H.M. Forces were firmly rejected. The recruiting officers told
me I was nowhere near 19 – in language that was crude but
eloquent.

But on one wintry day in November 1914 I was actually
accepted for the 15th Battalion Royal Welsh Fusiliers, known as
the London-Welsh.

I had no Welsh connections of any kind. My new soldier
comrades were real dyed-in-the-wool Welshmen who for
various reasons had been living in London. Most of them spoke
Welsh. They accepted me in friendly and cultured fashion, but
they quickly and outspokenly exposed that I was *not* Welsh.
But this did not worry me much. I was on my way to France.
And in the meantime the girls had a nice smile for boys in khaki
– apart from the fact that a uniform could save you getting a
white feather from an unduly patriotic female.

The growing Unit assembled every day in the grounds of
Grays Inn, London and we all returned to our homes every
night. To recompense for this burden on our private finances
our pay was (temporarily) raised to three shillings (15p) a day.
The basic pay was one shilling (5p) a day.

After about a month of parades playing at soldiers among the
fallen Autumn leaves in Grays Inn our as yet incomplete battalion was conveyed to Llandudno in North Wales. There, on
arrival at the railway station, a band played *Land of my
Fathers*. Welsh people are justly renowned for their musical
appreciation and I later found them give expression to it in
circumstances which ranged from the appalling to the exquisite.
This melodic reception at Llandudno was therefore an emotive
and patriotic affair, and for the first time I felt a real sense of
guilt as a gate-crasher.

We were billeted in hotels and boarding houses. The troops
were received almost as holiday visitors. They occupied ordinary bedrooms and were catered for by the hotel waitresses and
general staff.

As the weeks went by in Llandudno, however, it became obvious that the supply of real Welshmen exiled in London had run out and fell grievously below the number required for battalion strength. More and more non-Welshmen were therefore accepted, including a fair number of unmistakable London cockneys. Finally, pure Welshmen formed only the proud nucleus of the battalion. On the Sunday morning church parades, for example, when the sergeant-major had to separate the various religious denominations, he would yell:

"London-Welsh Battalion. 'Shun. Fall out the *Jews*" and then proceed to sort out the rest.

As almost always happens among bodies of men drawn from various areas with different interests there were several partisan or sectarian disputes, a few of which ended in punch-ups. They were always kept in rigid check by the battalion noncommissioned officers, the higher rankers among them being regular soldiers of the peace-time army. These sergeants and sergeant-majors could quickly cut down to size the most rebellious and ferocious recruits without inflicting any kind of direct physical punishment. Corporal punishment certainly could be applied, notoriously the tying of a culprit to a gun-carriage wheel, but this was very rarely imposed and was later forbidden altogether.

Discharge from the Army was delightfully simple to obtain in those early days of the war while man-power was abundant. I remember a London Cockney among us who became the battalion bugler, an appointment which did not seem to have matured because of any outstanding musical ability. One icy December morning his uncertain but strident *Reveille*, the hated military waking signal, reverberated around the Welsh hills at 4.30 a.m. instead of 5.30 a.m. and thus winkled all the Llandudno area troops out of bed one hour too early. The ensuing avalanche of abuse put an ignominious end to his melodic career. As a result he "worked his ticket" (jargon at that time for obtaining an absolute discharge from the Army) soon after. His justification; colour blindness. In civil life he was – a colour printer!

Before long a battalion notice appeared inviting suitable volunteers to form a Divisional Cyclist Company. Preference would be given to those knowing something about maps and one or more foreign languages. As I had a rudimentary knowledge of German and an acquaintance with maps (I had been the touring secretary of a cycling club) I was accepted for the new Cyclist unit.

14

The sketchy knowledge of the German language followed my employment for three years in the London office of the A.E.G., the German electrical giant. At the end of 1914 I was on a lone cycling holiday in Belgium and was in Antwerp when the European rumpus began. Quitting Antwerp with difficulty I managed to get a passage on an old tramp steamer making for Grimsby. When I reached the A.E.G. office in London I found that my boss, a German, had returned like a shot to the Fatherland for military service. He belonged to the Uhlan regiment and I often pictured him uniformed and complete with the traditional helmet that had the mortar-board looking contraption on top.

I immediately volunteered for the British army, but not because the A.E.G. was in any hurry to get rid of me. On the contrary, and astonishingly, they actually managed to pay my salary until December 1914 when they got through a letter to me from which I quote:

December 4, 1914

"You will recollect that when we expressed our desire to supplement your Army pay. . . .
The attitude of manufacturing concerns and the general public, in this country (Britain), is unfortunately of such a nature . . . and we are in consequence obliged to inform you that the allowance paid to you will cease at the close of this year. It is with regret etc. etc."

More than 45 years later (1960 in fact) I was in Frankfurt-on-Main on business and noticed that the A.E.G. had made its headquarters there. Its original *Hochhaus* in Berlin had inconveniently fallen in the Russian zone after the last war. Being very curious to know if my pre-1914 German boss had survived I called at the Frankfurt office. He had: and they gave me his address – in South Africa. Obviously moved by my reappearance the A.E.G. hurriedly arranged a kind of V.I.P. luncheon in honour, so they nicely and generously put it, of their oldest employee then present, which I suppose I was. In my informal, off-the-cuff few words of thanks for their fine lunch and amiable attention I paid tribute to their magnanimous treatment of an enemy alien by paying me full salary for five months while I fought against their country. But, I regretted to point out, there was a seamy side to their testimonial. And although I put it over to them in good fun, my story was absolutely true. One grey, chilly and mournful dawn in the trenches after a

15

night during which much explosive hardware was exchanged, I wearily sat down on the trench firestep.

"Look out," yelled someone next to me. "You are sitting on a bloody stick bomb."

This heavy grenade fixed to a wooden handle (to facilitate throwing it) had lain directly underneath me for hours yet failed to explode. Boldly imprinted on the handle was the manufacturer's trade mark A.E.G.!

"So you see," I chided my hosts, "you did your best to kill me." As I had hoped, they took my leg-pull in all good humour.

My new Unit, the 38th (Welsh) Divisional Cyclist company began its history at Conway, North Wales. The bicycles, when they did eventually arrive, were incredibly heavy. They were made to fold with the idea of being portable. But the genius responsible for their construction must have imagined he was working for a tribe of Herculian cyclists because it was only by help from at least two other people that the folded machine could be hoisted and strapped to one's back. So in practice the brain wave was a waste of time and in due course these crazy vehicles were replaced by cycles of standard design – a cumbersome design, however, which broke the hearts of those club cyclist stylists among us.

III

BIENVENUE EN FRANCE

After a few months "training" at Winchester which, because of the shortage of ammunition and weapons, included about only six practise rifle shots, the hour came to leave for France, and the trenches. We were cooped up in the ship's hold until dawn, when we were allowed on deck and saw the French coast gradually loom into view. It did not look at all inviting in that cold and foggy daybreak.

We disembarked at Le Havre. Two days at the base camps there left us with no illusions about life for the troops in France and what was in store for us. Bell tents in the mud with 24 (or more) human feet (in boots) to the centre pole when the occupants were asleep; one tin of Maconochies among five men for rations (a tin of cooked meat and vegetables which, although undoubtedly nutritious, was to be cursed because of its endless appearance on the menu); and our first real acquaintance with lice and other pests. These few chilling precursors of coming trials were, however, to be playful trifles compared with things to come.

After two days at Le Havre we were moved off, the first of a multitude of journeys in France that we came to accept with a dumb and listless indifference. If the wheres and whys of these moves were ever known to our immediate masters – the sergeants and corporals – they also couldn't care less – or so it seemed. No one ever told the privates . . . but very few privates really wanted to know! On this first move from Le Havre we had our early experience of conveyance by French wartime rail in the *40 hommes ou 5 cheveaux* container wagons – with the makeweight that our trucks had to take about 50 *hommes* apiece. If prisoners of war were transported in such conditions it would be considered inhumane treatment!

We detrained at St. Omer, the famous base town of the British Expeditionary Force. The idea was to collect our cycles at the railhead there.

"Your bloody bikes have gone on the wrong line," said the

transport sergeant at the railhead. A wait of some hours in heavy rain and then our Commanding Officer gallantly decided that his instructions to proceed demanded fulfilment, mounted or afoot. And as there were apparently no spare trains, and for all he knew our cycles had gone back to Le Havre, he ordered his 250 bikeless warriors to footslog it to the appointed destination, a desolate hamlet called Glominghem. This unplanned tramp with full equipment – about 20 miles in driving rain and sleet – reduced a fairly sprightly batch of 250 young men to a bedraggled, sodden, muddy, tired, hungry and blasphemous rabble by the end of the long day and night.

The famous fraternization between British and German front line troops on Christmas Day 1914 lingered longer in the minds of the men than the High Command considered decent.

It was generally accepted that the Germans took the initiative in this sociable interlude. Anyway, what was sure is that the British Tommies cordially and spontaneously reciprocated the gesture and, allowing for all circumstances and the lack of Christmas amenities in No-Mans-Land, a good time was had by all. But it appeared that this kind of goings on was anathema and intolerable to British Headquarters. Such antics were unsafe for Belligerency. These ideas could lead to a breakdown of the war, even cause peace. And so on the approach of Christmas Day of the following year, 1915, a stern edict was circulated to all fighting line Units forbidding any repetition of such peaceful overtures. To make sure of it the British artillery was ordered to lay down a bombardment, Christmas notwithstanding. In anger at this anti-Yuletide and unexpected hostility the Germans, of course, retaliated. And as up to that time they had much the advantage in situation, munitions, and trench fortifications, the British, as usual, had the worst of the exchange. That meant, of course, those British who manned the trenches and wanted nothing more than a quiet Christmas; those who disagreed were probably enjoying a fairly merry Christmas – at Amiens, or some other base haven well behind.

On that particular Christmas night, while all this artillery duel and general shooting was going on, we cyclists were assigned the job of receiving and guiding a Unit of Welsh Regiment artillery from an advance railhead to its up-the-line destination. By night, and exposed, it was imperative to take these Units by the shortest practical routes from railheads to destinations; but various bridges and other features on the different ways would not always take the weight and size of the artillery chariots, limbers and other transport. It was therefore

18

of great importance that the routes be carefully surveyed before we started leading a Unit, which itself could easily stretch out for a mile. A bogged or obstructed truck could jam the lot for the night and leave the whole stranded Unit a field-day target for the enemy artillery when daylight broke. This night's route was unusually tortuous and the task of coaxing the columns along narrow, slimy, shell-holed and bombarded lanes in inky blackness may be better imagined than described. The rain-soaked drivers swore and roared as they tried to control their horses which reared in terror at the vivid explosions of enemy shells on this hallowed eve. Dawn was not far off before we shepherded the last of our charges to their appointed sites. And when we could finally report Mission Accomplished it included no seasonal greetings to our Top Brass who had caused us such a hell of a Christmas night.

The great idea was to use us cyclists as express cavalry on wheels immediately we met the enemy in France. But since such mounted mobility was seriously obstructed by the trench systems which were solid from the North Sea to Switzerland, we wheeled warriors were perforce dismounted on reaching the trenches where we had to operate as footslogging infantry instead. Alternatively, our Company was detailed for night operations of various kinds in the trenches. Every evening at dusk we would cycle the mile or two from our bases to the specified sector of the trenches which needed repair or attention or actual fighting support. Often this would mean repairing or erecting barbed wire or other obstructions or dealing with corpses in No Man's Land. Those who survived many an uncomfortable hour between the front lines can recall an uncanny similarity to what our post-war science-fiction artists imagine the Martian landscape to look like. The No Man's Land of the 1914–18 European War was a feature peculiar to that war because other campaigns did not produce such static concentrations as four years of stationary hammering at each other. No one lingered a moment longer than was vital in N.M.L. And no wonder. Unexploded munitions, enemy snipers, deep mine craters and shell holes full of slimy water, rotting corpses, others grievously wounded but left for dead were grim companions. Survival by night in N.M.L. was a technique of reacting to the constant alternations of brilliance and blackness. When the night sky over N.M.L. was made brighter than day by the frequently soaring Verey Lights, those exposed below would freeze into immobility so that their bodies might merge into the ghastly still-life formations grotesquely silhouetted by the glare of the rockets. The

19

slightest movement would attract sudden death from snipers. This made the operations of working parties a matter of stop-go fits and starts. Both sides had machine guns fixed on targets against which it was merely a matter of pulling the trigger. No aim necessary. When, as often happened, the Germans had their working parties out in N.M.L., as well as ours, it was a case of Live and Let Live. Neither interfered with the other while both were out between the lines, but as soon as one side had crawled back it behoved the other to regain the comparative shelter of its own front trench before the enemy gunners had a go.

Of the several criminally idiotic iniquities inflicted on British troops there was perhaps none more lunatic than the compulsory polishing of the brass buttons on tunics and greatcoats. Some moronic high ranker at British H.Q. decided that this polishing business was essential for morale and discipline in the 1914–18 war. Although the vital rule for remaining alive in N.M.L. during Verey Light treatment was to maintain a paralyzed stance, anything bright was most conspicuous. All British N.M.L. operators therefore have some frightening memories of presenting scintillating outlines in the form of five gleaming tunic buttons and four smaller pocket buttons. The German gunners naturally did not overlook such gratuitous targets.

In some sectors of Flanders, trenches were not practicable and so both sides built up breast works of sandbags above ground level. The area was low-lying and waterlogged. Such was the terrain around Neuve Chapelle, famous for the first planned and major British attack, and where it is said we lost more men in the first day's assault than we lost in the whole of the three years' Boer War in South Africa.

The German trench system there lay on slightly higher ground than ours. This meant that the British had to maintain a crude but constant drainage flow between the lines and beyond, or else wallow in a permanent stagnant, slimy and insanitary morass. And so one night found me as one of a working party ordered to N.M.L. to clear a blockage in that "drainage" system. The cause of that blockage was dead bodies of the British, killed at the Battle of Neuve Chapelle. Most of the British dead were Indian soldiers who had been brought to France early in the war. Killed, they had fallen into a former German communication trench and had rotted. Putrefaction had set in and the job of clearing the corpses was indeed a revolting and gruesome task. Legs and arms would pull completely away. Shells had torn into the carcases, and rats had not missed their opportunities. The stench of dead flesh hung around us, either in fact or imagination, for days after. It took us all night to clear the congestion, during which the Germans hammered us with copious deliveries from their varied armoury.

It was officially admitted that the Battle of Neuve Chapelle failed because of "the inability of the commander of the 4th Army Corps to bring his reserve brigades more speedily into action". The assault is said to have been planned because the stationary warfare was beginning to affect the morale of the troops (of which side was not clear). So this officially described "flat, marshy, dyke-chequered" sector was chosen for the first ambitious British attack.

IV

LICE, SCABIES, FLIES and RATS

We soon became too well acquainted with that loathsome para-
site the body louse. Rats, the itch mite (scabies), and the common fly were additional pests that 1914–1918 troops in Europe
had to live with, but the louse was by far the most ubiquitous
and offensive. Nobody in the war area dodged lice. Ordinary
troops living cheek by jowl naturally attracted the greatest
attention. The only occasions upon which louse bitings ceased
from the neck downwards were the rare moments when showers
or makeshift baths were possible. Our heads were never free,
because hair harboured its own specie of lice which laughed at
hot water, brushes or any other supposed onslaught.

All places where men gathered were infected. The trench
dugouts were particularly lousy. Although a combination of
water, slime and often ice might seem an inhospitable rendezvous for any land based organism, the old mattresses, sandbags,
sacks and "curtains" furnishing the trench shelters were
treasured by trillions of lice and rats as idyllic restaurant-
lounges. The old farm barns just behind the lines that served as
billets for the troops during "rest" periods were equally lousy.
Men would sit on the straw covered barn floor, with their backs
to the wall, playing lighted candles around the lice-clusters in
the seams of their tunic collars. At first it seemed that the
misery of having to tolerate these pests was limited to the perpetual biting, itching and consequent scratching. But it later
became painfully evident that lice were the cause of more sinister effects.

In addition to the ordinary maladies that would predictably
affect armies, especially under the insanitary conditions common to World War I, there emerged an ever increasing incidence of a disease which had not been known, or at any rate
never been diagnosed, before that war. For want of better identification they called it Trench Fever, although it was no more
connected with trenches than anywhere else where the troops
assembled. At first some army doctors confused it with rheuma-
tism or lumbago. Others gave it the name "Trench Shin", be-

cause this new malady gave pains of varying intensity in both shins. This is probably where the misnomer Trench Fever originated – the result, so it was thought, of standing for long periods in wet trenches. But when specific tests later proved that this fever did not belong to any known disease branches, it was candidly labelled P.U.O. (Pyrexia of Uncertain Origin.)

There appeared to be two distinct forms, however. One where, at the onset, patients ran a temperature of 102–103°F. for three days, followed by an apparent recovery – until the sixth, seventh and eighth days when the disease recurred with added severity. The other form early produced a high temperature and intense sweating. It lasted just five days – in fact the Germans called it the "Five Day Fever".

Alarmed by the increasing incidence of Trench Foot all over the Western Front and its serious effect on Army strength, the British made determined efforts to solve and combat the evil. They were fairly certain it was a blood disease transferred somehow from one person to another. Researchers named Davis and Weldon first suspected lice as the carriers and so, where possible, soldiers' clothing was subjected to 80°F. dry heat, a temperature well above the degree thought necessary at that time to kill lice and eggs. From Salonica, where our forces also had a serious share of Trench Fever it was discovered that no infection at all came from troops transferred *from* the Dardanelles. It was all brought by the troops moved from France. But the disease spread and grew apace, and the mystery of its transmission remained. By now thoroughly alarmed, the War Office directed research to be undertaken by a clinic at Hampstead specially established for the study of obscure diseases. And as 1917 went by without isolating the culpable organism, the War Office appointed an official Trench Fever Committee which concentrated on the possibility of transmission by lice.

In one experiment an elderly volunteer lay on an old mattress in an improvised dugout and submitted to a biting orgy by 250 lice which had all previously gorged on Trench Fever sufferers. But he emerged quite pure and unaffected. There followed 23,000 bites in other experiments, but they produced no sign of Trench Fever, and it became evident that simple lice bites were not the answer.

Inspiration and excreta are hardly connonatives, but one certainly led to the other in eventually finding the clue. Someone became inquisitive about the dark brown dust left in the boxes that contained the experimental lice. It was also pointed out that elderly people – such as the volunteer guinea pigs used so

23

far – would not scratch the lice bites as younger soldiers, because their skin was nowhere near so hard as their elders. So the next experiment was the rubbing of the excreta into actual scratch wounds, and the result was – Trench Fever! Over 500 experiments with the "dark brown dust" produced the same result – Trench Fever after eight days. Thus the cause was discovered: but the war finished without a cure. A drug giving a specific result (such as Salvarsan – "606" – on syphilis spirochete) as well as various thyroid preparations were introduced, but the cure and elimination of Trench Fever eluded solution. Mothers, wives and sweethearts sent their men all kinds of ointments and preparation in tubs, bottles and tins, but these seemed only to stimulate the vermin. A standing joke was that the lice would wait for the "treatments" much as garden birds might wait for the morning bread crumbs.

Another pest, prevalent to an unwelcome extent, and even more detested, was the itch mite. This caused Scabies. Under the microscope it looked as horribly grotesque as anything nature could contrive, and the fact that the female of this unlovely species grovelled just under the surface of one's skin was fortunately unknown to the many thousands who contracted this foul complaint. This detestable little wanderer would feed and frolic, on and under our bare bodies, and the offending female would deposit her eggs in batches immediately below the skin surface. This of course caused the human host promptly to scratch vigorously and repeatedly, which soon punctured his skin and facilitated the process of egg transmission until large areas of the body were infected. The sufferer contracted Trench Fever automatically, even more severely than the lice infected strain. The fever plus vast patches of bleeding abrasions and scabs which he had to endure, made the patient's misery easier imagined than described. Scabies was so awfully contagious that notification and isolation were compulsory, whether identification happened in the battle line or not. I contracted scabies in the trenches during the freezing January of 1917. With hundreds of others I was clapped in an improvised Isolation Camp just behind the lines. Hourly sulphur baths was the treatment there, and after some weeks the ravages subsided. Whether *sarcoptes scabiei* (itch mite) succumbed to the sulphur I do not know. But I do know that the disease was one of those scourges of the 1914–18 war which grew to a menace never fully revealed.

As for rats ... well, of course, they were everywhere. But although the troops thoroughly detested them they were not regarded as so sinister as the other pests. In fact we learnt to put up with them in a way we could not tolerate lice and flies. The trench lines, dugouts and latrines etc. were paradises for rats. A night sentry doing his lonely, nervy, one-hour vigil on the front-line firestep, peering anxiously into the black mysteries of No-Mans-Land, where all objects "moved" no matter how inanimate they actually were, was often scared out of his pants by a rat or two scampering over his poised rifle on the trench parapet. And the scraping and rattling of rats in between the lines would frequently cause both sides to blaze away in fear of a trench raid. The knowledge of what was giving the rats such a fine feed in No-Mans-Land did not increase our affection for them either. In the old barns where we "rested" by night when out of the trenches, the rats began their expeditions as soon as the candles were snuffed. Any food not securely submerged somewhere would be gone by the morning. It seemed that one rat was first sent out as a scout. If and when he gave the O.K. a general advance would ensue. Men who were not too tired would lie in wait with bayonets poised and there would be many thrusts. But very seldom a score. The rat flea could of course be the cause of terrible scourges, but the Western Front seemed to escape that aspect. Although of the same family, the rat flea did not relish humans unless some rat indisposition caused a shortage of sustenance. Then the fleas would have a go at anything.

Flies were a menace and a great nuisance, especially around trench latrines. These earthworks were unavoidably rather shallow and, being subject to frequent upheaval by enemy shelling, were an open attraction to the fly world. Whereas several aspects of trench life were live-and-let-live examples of Anglo-German War Relations (or rather Tommy-Fritz understanding) lavatory emplacements were targets for belligerency. Take just one example: it was considered a dirty trick for either side to pummel the trench systems while the "mess orderlies" were struggling to bring up the breakfast rations of hot tea, coffee and eats – unless of course an attack was in progress or imminent. The loos, alas, which were delineated with accuracy by both sides, enjoyed no immunity from the missiles of war. On the contrary they were deliberate targets. So in addition to the necessity of attendance at the loo being a very hazardous function, the apprehensive occupant would also be enveloped in hordes of filthy flies who settled *everywhere*. In these days, the 70's, there are surely chemical or other means of dealing with such dangers, but in the 1914–18 war flies must have caused ravages of a variety and scope impossible to be assessed.

V

"GERMAN 'JACK JOHNSONS' AND SHRAPNEL GALORE . . ."

From February 1916 we began going nightly to a sinister location known as Givenchy, near La Bassee, a sector to become hatefully familiar to us Cyclists for a long time to come. We approached it by way of an unromantic stretch of water, the La Bassee Canal, and then negotiated tracks and communication trenches which the troops had named in the geographical order of the London scene – Westminster Bridge Road, Lambeth Road, Vauxhall Bridge Road, etc.

Nightly we cycled to Givenchy by way of the canal towpath which the German artillery knew with damnable precision. Cyclists were sometimes blown off the side into the dirty water after being knocked about by shell blasts.

We would join the canal near the town of Bethune, of which only rubble remained by the end of 1918. Its rebuilt and placid successor of today belies the tales its forerunner could tell of its World War I days. Bethune was the advance marshalling and control point for those holocausts to become notorious as Neuve Chapelle, Festubert, Laventie, Givenchy, Quinchy Brickstacks and Loos, etc. It was a kind of mecca for all units of the then far-flung British Empire. Although its strategic importance attracted daily bombardments of varying intensity from the German artillery and planes, Bethune's bustle and activity was seldom hampered for long. Its famous Red Lamp establishment maintained operations undaunted by enemy high explosives. Men of all nations and creeds supporting the Allies, white, black and other skins, queued more or less patiently for its physical welcome. The average lady on its staff was said to "service" a battalion of clients (about 1,000 men) before "retiring pale but proud" as one famous war historian put it.

The original Givenchy village itself lay around an innocent looking turn in the road known to the Tommies as Windy Corner. Had this nickname implied nothing more gusty than wind there would have remained a good fewer wooden crosses in France. Because the German machine gunners were able to enfilade this lethal curve in the road (and it was the only way of entering or leaving Givenchy) one negotiated it in daylight only in dire necessity, in breathless haste and – in a state of tremendous "wind up". As a matter of unhappy convenience, the shelled remains of a building by Windy Corner did service as the army mortuary, and more often than not its gruesome occupants were in full view of anyone scurrying round this sinister corner.

The Givenchy sector lay on one of the very few ridges in this part of France. Although only a minor ridge, it was sufficient to invite the field engineers of both sides to play at burying explosive depth charges under each other's trenches. This was euphemistically known as Mining Operations. Before the war ended, however, the whole of both German and British trench systems in this sector was elaborately tunnelled for the emplacement of powerful mines, all ready to blow. At will, either Army Commands could, and did, press buttons and detonate localities at least as spacious as an average big village and they were the most dreadful explosive operations of the war. And so it was that trench life at Givenchy was kind of dishonest and deceitful. For fair periods it could all be blissfully serene – more quiet and peaceful than in times of peace because there were not the ordinary noises of prewar days. And then, with unnerving suddenness, a square mile of earth would rock and convulse, followed by a deafening and prolonged roar. If it were night time – and because of its more shattering effect on the senses it usually was – that roar was accompanied by vivid red flashes and stabs. In their glare scores of sandbags could be seen hurtling upwards and returning earthwards; bodies as well! Depending on just where the mine was sprung, both sides would at once be concerned as to who was to occupy the crater. A set-to with small arms and machine guns would begin the fiendish confrontation. Then the light and medium artillery of both sides would have a go. The flashes would provide the spotters for the big howitzers and long range cannons the opportunity to pin-point the opposing gun positions and they would then add their heavyweight hardware to the inferno. By that time the front line men would be fighting for the crater and, eventually, either the Germans or the British would "win" the big hole and hang on to it indefinitely. Official reports would record the capture of one of these craters "for the loss of *only* 60 men". The italics are mine. Possession of these craters was thereafter an expensive "prize" because their unfortunate defenders were terribly exposed and their casualty rate scored a high even among the appalling mortality records of World War I.

I had a reputation for losing things, which I must confess was not unjustified. In the course of my service I probably lost every single item of my kit and accoutrements – including my rifle and my bayonet. One night my unit was ordered to the trenches at Givenchy in support of a Wiltshire battalion, and I was detailed as a runner. In the absence of today's sophisticated techniques, the human messenger was then the most reliable means of communication. To be a runner implied no running. Shell holes full of watery slime and barbed wire were but some obstacles to speed: the rank of crawler would have more precisely described the appointment. However, my accommodation (while awaiting the order to "run") was a tunnel in a trench leading to the commanding officer's dug-out. In the event of enemy attack my job was to send up green rockets and then "run" with a message to troops in support trenches and beseech reinforcements. The first night was quiet. The commanding officer, being a nice chap, sent ample victuals (and rum) to me in my lonely, dim and damp lair. But the following night an enemy mine suddenly raised hell, and the war engines of both sides roared into operation. My little tunnel, with me in it, rocked and twisted and, among other inconveniences, my candle was blown out. There may be several shades of darkness, but I can recall nothing blacker than a narrow tunnel in loose, wet earth with all light suddenly extinguished.

"Fire the green rockets, Runner" shouted the commanding officer. In fact he had yelled that several times, but the noises of war were predominant.

"Yes sir. Will do, sir. Right away", I obediently answered while I rummaged in my pockets for another candle. I found one. *But I had lost the rockets.* I am afraid the democratic kind of *esprit de corps* hitherto prevailing twixt commanding officer and his humble runner was abruptly ruptured. The officer was, however, sporty enough eventually to assume that the mine blast had swept my rockets away.

VI

MINES AND "MINNIES"

As the months wore on and the trench lines became almost static, both sides improved and added to their own particular brands of inter trench missiles – a variety of deadly short-range weapons which ranged from explosives as small as walnuts to gigantic canisters of detonative devilry. I think our pride in that line was what our chaps called a Flying Pig because it looked like one in transit. Its huge size and content must have been most unwelcome to the Germans. But in my opinion the supreme terror in this malevolent endeavour was the German *Minenwerfer,* a trench mortar rocket weighing up to about 190 lb. A dull pop would be the only sound that signalled one of these terrible missiles leaving the German operators. At night it would hover aloft with a red glow at its tail, 100ft or so up. Wriggling and wavering it left those below with very little idea as to where exactly it would fall, but its explosion would reach them with more or less impact wherever it landed. So you would press your tense, cold and tired body hard against the wet and muddy sandbags and await the crash – if you lived to hear it. There would be a roaring blast and a lurid flash, with earthquaking accompaniment. If you were lucky and your anatomy remained intact you could then fearfully await and watch up for the next one.

World War I produced diabolical contrivances which might have caused more killing than the *Minenwerfer* (mine thrower) but in my experience – and I became acquainted with most of the lethal paraphernalia in vogue – the "Minnie" was Terror No. 1 among the nerve shattering weapons endured by our fellows in the trenches.

During one such "Minnie" bombardment at Givenchy one wintry night I was doing my one-hour-on watch on the firestep, alone. Although there was more risk to be in dugouts during Minenwerfer *strafes,* men not on watch duty would often remain inside their "shelters" and risk the greater danger in return for a fitful sleep out of the rain and cold. Someone, a corporal as a rule, was supposed to maintain occasional contact with the trench sentries during their lonely vigils. But a trench selected by the Germans for concentrated bombardment hardly provided amenities for ceremonial liaison. Anyway, on this particular night a "Minnie" blasted me off the firestep and left me half buried. I have no clear recollection of being "recovered" but I eventually came to, bruised, dazed and benumbed, in some underground cellars which served as a dressing station in our support lines. I had suffered no flesh wounds but I was a whimpering, trembling and plaintive object, unsteady in gait and incoherent in speech; and due to remain so for some weeks to come. The slightest sudden noise gave me paroxysms of distress. The mere thought of trenches evoked utter terror.

I was copiously treated with the pills and tablets that served as tranquillizers at that time and after a few days these certainly reduced my agitation. But when the time came to release me from medical attention it must have been very obvious that I was not yet fit for the firing line. So I was seconded to a detachment for mining work *under* the German trenches.

Trench warfare was notorious for providing appalling jobs, but I remember none more abominable, dirty, eerie, exhausting and fearful than underground sapping in World War I. The point of descent to these subterranean workings was usually a shaft dug just behind our front-line trench. On average it would go down about 50 ft and then, sideways or up and under the German trench lines. The shafts and tunnels gave crawling and wriggling space only. Efficient draining being impracticable there was always a dripping wetness, and you were given oil-skin garments to wear which were noted more for the discomfort they caused than the water they kept out. The first man to descend would squirm to the end of the tunnel so far as it was cut and then proceed to extend it by scraping out the wet clay, often with his hands, and put it in sandbags. When full, the sandbag would be dragged backwards to the shaft exit by the other men in the party who had also crawled down, behind and along, and thus formed a human chain in line astern.

The German miners would also be at the same game. For some reason our engineers always contrived to get their tunnels underneath the German tunnels, although the two were always uncomfortably near each other. Frequently there would be sudden and whispered orders to cease all movement and remain utterly paralysed while a listening session, with very sensitive microphones, took place.

"Jerry is working less than four bloody feet above us" murmured our sergeant on one occasion. We could hear the taps and scrapes without the aid of microphones. "Keep your eyes skinned" added the sergeant – in case a German digging tool should penetrate our tunnel wall. In that dreaded event, the theoretical routine was to lob a couple of hand grenades into the enemy apartment and then get the hell out of it just as fast as you could wriggle your oilskin-enclosed body along a blind, slimy aperture some 60ft down in the clay morass. These enemy penetrations did happen. I remember our chaps once digging into a German mine gallery and withdrawing 2,000 lb of the enemy's explosive. But this was planned and not an accident. Whatever was going on, both sides would almost continuously try to blow in the opposing shaftheads with mortar artillery, invariably with dire consequences to those down below when a hit was on target. When an underground mine was actually detonated there would generally be some luckless tunnellers of the other side working below, and there would be no uncertainty about their horrible fate.

This, then, was the Army's idea of a spell of convalescence from "Minnie"-shock as far as I was concerned. Nevertheless, I did slowly improve and in due course was returned to my own cyclist company which continued its role of support operations to any hard pressed units on various fronts in that sector.

Along the many miles from roughly Laventie to Arras, both sides operated stationary warfare for most of 1917. This gave the artillery range finders the opportunity to pin-point their targets with guaranteed accuracy. Any specified 30 square yards of trenches could receive the *concentrated* missiles from guns of all calibres and characteristics and in some parts these guns would be almost wheel to wheel over large areas. Yet you could, in safety, watch from 150ft distant the target area of say 30 square yards being pulverized and its unfortunate occupants annihilated, so precise became these fiendish cannonades. No other campaign has produced such density of fire power.

Trench raiding parties then became the mode. The strength of those taking part could be as large as 250 men formidably armed, but the favourite plan was a dozen or so fellows with blackened faces and armed only with a bayonet, a cosh and wirecutters. They would squirm through the obstructions, shell holes, craters and barbed wire of No-Man's-Land, often floundering deep in slime *en route*. Those who succeeded in reaching the enemy front trench would, if they could, cosh unconscious one unsuspecting German sentry and drag him back alive to our lines for "intelligence" interrogation. We were told that these operations yielded invaluable evidence as to *which* enemy regiment was *where* and gave reliable clues to German strategic movements. In view of the abundant secret intelligence that was available, even in those days, the explanation was certainly not swallowed by those who had to do the raiding; and I never ever met just one of the legendary devil-may-care characters who were reputed to enjoy that kind of operation. There was nothing in the least noble, dashing or romantic about the average night trench raid, and the cost in lives was outrageous.

These static fronts also made ideal testing grounds for the ever increasing variety of new tactics for killing each other. The consequent novel ideas and implements were often tried out in conjunction with a trench raiding party whose mission was to ascertain and report on the effect of the new devices. One night at Annequin the Royal Engineers tried out boiling oil. For a long time the Germans had played with flame as a weapon, using an appliance they called *Flammenwerfer* (flame thrower). It was alarming, but as the flame was usually projected horizontally it went harmlessly over the top and past you provided you were in a trench or beneath it. Not so our boiling oil. Rocketed over in large containers, it burst a few yards *above* the enemy's trenches. The liquid oil then shot down in flaming dollops, and we could hear screams from the burning Germans. Our raiding party then went over ... and thus another nightly episode added its quota of tortured and mutilated males to the maniacal procession. I personally never came across or heard of boiling oil since that one night at Annequin until a few years after the war, when I happened to see the obituary notice of a certain colonel who claimed to have devised it. It stays in my mind as the zenith of human devilry. ...

VII

AN AGREEABLE INTERLUDE

By the Autumn of 1917, the Italians, our allies then, were in trouble. Following their defeat on the Caporetto sector, where the Austro-German forces claimed to have netted 30,000 prisoners, the Italians were in full retreat.

There was much fighting on the Italian front during the Spring and early Summer of 1917 and some of the unhappy consequences to the Italian army provoked dissension. among the military chiefs as well as providing propaganda for the anti-war and pacifist groups. The latter were far more active in Italy than could be said of the other Western Allies. Something approaching mutiny broke out among new forces which had just reached the firing line. The men shouted rebellious slogans in favour of ending the war and there were several "unfortunate incidents." These fresh troops had been assembled and trained in an area notorious for its seditious publicity and anti-war demonstrations. The overall disquiet caused General Cadorna, the Italian military chief, to send an official note to his Government protesting that not enough was being done to suppress the flow of pacifist propaganda which was having such an insidious effect on the morale of the Italian army.

According to *The Times,* the Italian ministerial system then prevailing was "not fair to the Italian people" which was "almost at the mercy of those who preach pacifism, pro-Germanism and all the other isms . . ."

The Italian military position became sufficiently serious in July 1917 to necessitate Allied conferences and discussions, in the course of which it was decided to divert reinforcements to the Italian front by October 1917.

In the meantime a further embarrassment for the Allies was the famous Papal Peace Note of August 1917 by Pope Benedict XV, addressed from the Vatican "to the Heads of the Belligerent Peoples". The Allied countries generally stigmatised the note as a propaganda victory for Germany in her alleged drive for Peace in order to avoid certain defeat. More damaging for the Allies was its serious undermining of the already lowered morale of the Italian forces and the people. The Papal Note was published at just the time when Italy was about to launch its maximum military effort and they could not conceal the disturbing effect it had on the army.

The old proverb about the ill wind blowing someone some good was a truism as far as I felt concerned. It was hard luck for the Italians but the Italian front turned out to be a halcyon retreat and a holiday from the barrages, mud, privations and death that attended trench life in France. My unit was one of the fortunate troops to be chosen as part of a relief force to be dispatched in great haste from the British front in France.

En route by rail through France to Italy I saw the French Riviera for the first time and from the train it looked as though no whisper of war had reached it. Arriving in Italy we made our way to the front on our bikes. By this time I was a cyclist Lewis Gunner.

It was made known to us in the way that information reached ordinary soldiers – "now you know it, keep your bloody mouths shut" – that the Italian troops had become "disaffected". It seemed to us that this was a euphemism for mutiny, if that's the word for a disaffection ranging from lethargy and apathy to sheer disobedience. When we eventually approached to within about 30 miles of the advancing Austro-German enemy, the Italian soldiery were passing *through* us, the other way. All marching order had gone and they were just a fleeing rabble. I have not the slightest wish to be uncomplimentary in any way whatever in describing this. Rather will I accept – indeed I am *certain* – that some devastating circumstances had broken them, similar to reverses that have broken good soldiers of *every* nation at some time or other. But the fact remains. We, the British, eventually faced the enemy across the River Piavre: and without denying that our men would have put up very touch opposition had the necessity arisen, it was conceded that this River Piavre had most to do with halting the Austro-German thrust.

Novel to us were the very deep Italian trenches – so deep that we could not make out how any defenders down in them could possibly engage any attackers coming over the top. Anyway, there were now no Italians in these trenches and since they had largely served as lavatories we dug our own new earthworks.

As time went on we British were able to consolidate our positions and equipment but when we first reached the river we could only hurriedly dig in on our side and await the attack –

that never came. Heavy enemy air raids were our main distraction and they went on from dusk to dawn. The Lewis machine gun team to which I belonged was assigned almost nightly to aerial defence. The Italian anti-aircraft artillery would hammer away at the least suspicion of anything unusual in the sky but although they, and our many Lewis Gun teams, maintained a pretty incessant racket I never heard of a single enemy plane that fell to our fire. Planes crashed at a rate certainly alarming from the Austro-German angle, but engine failure, weather, and the many hazards of flying in those days were the causes. In fact the enemy airmen almost nightly swooped to roof top level to have a go at our guns, so contemptuous were they of our possible danger to them.

An unexpected problem for the British top brass was the potency of the cheap and plentiful Italian wine. In contrast to the anaemic French beer, which was universally called cat's piss by most British troops, a mess tin full of lively wine was obtainable in northern Italy for a Lira which in those days had the exchange rating of 6d. (2½p) Drunkenness – no other word for it I'm afraid – became so serious and widespread that the command issued an order placing all wine restaurants out of bounds for British troops. Squads of military police visited the cafes in order to ensure that this edict was obeyed. But these squads of military police often ended up drunk themselves.

VIII

TO HELL AGAIN

In March 1918, after three months of this relative holiday in Italy, came a sudden order recalling us to France, where the German onslaughts were posing a really serious menace. And so at the beginning of April 1918 the XIth Corps Cyclists, in which I was a Lewis Gunner of C Company, languished in delapidated and lousy farm barns at a hamblet called Hinges, roughly six miles behind our threatened lines. From Hinges we could be rushed to any spot on that sector which might be ruptured by German attack. There was very little doubt at that time that a rupture would indeed occur. We dozed fully clothed and endured a constant succession of false stand-to alarms every night from dusk to dawn. These stand-to alarms became so frequent and without issue that many of the chaps began turning out without full equipment, chancing another false alarm. And then of course it happened. The last stand-to, dawn of April 9, 1918, was *not* a false alarm.

"Files right: Move Off". The Cyclists' order to get going!

Many essentials were left behind, by far the most serious of which were panniers of Lewis Gun bullets.

Through a mist which blanketed a chilly, dismal dawn, we pedalled our heavy bikes to – destination uncertain. We ordinary Tommies had not the slightest notion, neither did we care. These many months of trench and nomad existence had reduced our outlook to a sheep-like vacuity. All destinations were alike; all equally cheerless. We dodged death and injury, if we could, in a listless, almost inattentive way, and accepted the hourly fact of other fellows being killed as merely just one of those things.

The Germans were now heavily shelling the roads, causing casualties and obstructions. Explosives always seemed and sounded more sinister in a mist or fog, for some reason. Our years in the fighting areas had accustomed us to artillery bombardments of varying intensities, but the king-size one now going on chilled the most hardened of us. Although we were yet three or four miles from the main barrage, its incessant, thunderous roar rocked the earth and disturbed the air for miles around. We knew very well that a major German attack was imminent somewhere in our sector.

That our destination that morning was a place called Lacouture was solely indicated by the fact that we were halted there. We stacked our cycles in the yard of a devastated farm after removing from them our packs, our Lewis Guns, and what ammunition we had not left behind. Missiles of all shapes and sizes were now exploding among us and as we were unavoidable exposed on open ground they were duly causing their quota of killing and wounding. Sudden death came to an old pal beside me. He was struck in the right temple by something and I became dumbly aware that head wounds can cause blood to spurt therefrom for several feet, like water from a hose. We made our way by following those in front of us to some improvised, strong defensive positions in the way of sandbagged firing points, camouflaged among some out-buildings, almost immediately adjoining the church of Lacouture. These positions showed signs of having recently been manned by others – Portuguese troops, so we later discovered.

The Germans now lifted their terrific barrage and lengthened its range to cause a metal curtain somewhere behind us. The only shells now falling on us were from the British side. Our gunners evidently assumed that all our troops had long been overwhelmed and if their shells hit anyone it could not be *us*. By this sequence of events we knew that the Germans had in fact launched their attack, although there was an entire absence of anything like news on the position. So we stoically assembled our Lewis Guns, placed the muzzles at the ready through the firing slots of the sandbagged "fort", and waited for what might come. No wordy orders or directions preceded or accompanied these operations, except for some banal comments, swearing, and ironic banter. Our gunners meanwhile crouched by their weapons for the kill. No officer mentioned who or what might come, where we were, or what we were to do in any given circumstances. No officer knew.

"Look out; Jerries!" suddenly shouted one of our chaps. And scrambling towards us, through barbed wire, debris, and newly made shell holes were troops sure enough. Dimly through the persistent mist and the smoke of bursting shrapnel (still from our own guns) we made out the unfamiliar helmets and uniforms.

"Let the bastards have it," yelled one of our corporals.

37

And about six of our Lewis Guns forthwith did just that.

We repeated this performance every time anything moved for the next half an hour or so. It seemed a funny kind of attack. Then, in the middle of another attempted advance by these troops, we heard our same corporal shout –

"Hold it lads. They're not Jerries. They're bloody Portuguese. The poor sods."

No one had told us anything about Portuguese.* We must have killed scores of the poor devils.

In this kind of confusion began what was to go down in history as the Battle of the Lys. It was the second of the tremendous German onslaughts during the Spring of 1918, by which they came nearer to reaching the Channel Ports and defeating the Allies than by any of their other efforts.

Confirmation that Portuguese troops were involved was finally made obvious by a few of them actually reaching our positions, where they took their places alongside us in the common defence. But their comrades – those who remained alive – were in full rout around us and to our rear. After one of the most terrible artillery hammerings ever known†, the Portuguese front simply disintegrated when the Germans attacked.

By now the enemy were paying much savage attention to the "stronghold" we cyclists occupied, and their thorough and sinister "wiping out" technique was in progress. Having advanced on either side well past us, our stubborn presence was a menace they could not allow to survive. So as well as the heaviest high explosives from their long range batteries and high velocity shrapnel (whizz-bangs) in saturation density from their lighter field guns, the Germans had crept sufficiently near to be able to dose our fort with *Minenwerfers*, their horrific mortars. Gas shells also arrived for makeweight. When these dropped they were usually recognizable by their dull thud upon detonation but in the present hullabaloo their arrival was overwhelmed by the din of all the other and noisier missiles. We were therefore caught without our gasmasks on. Fortunately, however, and for a reason I do not know, the gas failed to put many of us right out of action and the anti-gas pills we carried just about en-

---

* The Portuguese troops holding this sector were due to have been relieved by the British 50th Division but that operation could not take place. At 4.15 a.m. on April 9 the Germans subjected the Portuguese to a bombardment of an intensity never before equalled in trench warfare, and at 8.45 a.m. eight German divisions made the attack.

† In their own account of the action, the Germans record that they saturated the area with 30/40,000 gas shells.

abled most of us to keep going. But it took all one's instinct for self preservation to withstand the nausea and dull agony that followed a dose of war gas of any kind, however non-lethal.

The Germans had by now effectively surrounded us, and they were confident of annihilating us by bombardment rather than by hand-to-hand assault, which was sensible tactics on their part. As our firing positions faced the former German trenches – they were never intended for action in reverse – our sides and backs were now exposed to the enemy all around us. So a tense and uneasy watch for the expected attacks from uncertain quarters was to be our queasy predicament for the next phase.

In the event, however, the Germans were more nervous of our defence potential than our strength really warranted. So far it was a case of the small dog showing his teeth and ferociously barking. Not a single German soldier had yet showed himself. His advance troops were miles past us and he probably reckoned that half-an-hour's blanket blasting would reduce us to rubble. But it took him a lot longer than that, and the Germans extended and maintained their deluge of explosives until the bombardment was incessant. The sandbagged firing points manned by two of our Lewis Gun teams was once an ordinary room in an ordinary building which by now the cannonade was rocking as though it was a hammock. To the roar and blast of an exploding *Minenwerfer* both gun teams were suddenly enveloped in a cataclysm of disintegrating masonry, general debris, smoke and acrid fumes. The floor blew asunder, and the entire gun teams, 12 men, fell, almost neatly in the circumstances, in one lump down on to the cellar floor 10ft below.

"The bastards!" someone spluttered in the inky blackness. But no one was hurt, and after much spitting, coughing, and throat clearing from the filth and dust, they mutely and almost methodically re-erected themselves in firing positions.

The German battering continued without respite throughout the whole day and night of April 9/10. At dawn on April 10 we wearily but somewhat fearfully awaited a mass assault. The concentrated bombardment had taken a grievous toll. We survivors had passed a freezing and sleepless night. We were now entirely without food or drink. Our ammunition was nearly exhausted.

Then the enemy suddenly stopped all firing. This was almost always the sign of something to happen.

It did. No further than 10 yards from my gun muzzle a German steel helmet slowly arose from a trench. We riddled it, and in so doing we showed ourselves for the thoughtless idiots we were. That helmet encased no human head. It was just a decoy hoisted by the Germans to discover whether or not our fort was still manned. It was one of the oldest tricks in warfare and we should have known better than to give the game away. The price of our stupidity was a renewed shower of missiles on our lair.

As daylight began to break the Germans started using wheeled transport here and there and to make other movements in the distance. We sniped at anything that moved and inflicted obvious casualties and damage. The Germans who thus exposed themselves could have had no idea that any British were still holding out in such forward and isolated positions now that their advance infantry was a good ten miles past them. But those of the enemy immediately around us who were in the know – and they were evidently very plentiful – arranged speedy retaliation in the way of sniping, and they got several of us. While my No. 2 Gunner, whom we knew as Curly Baldwin, was fixing in firing position our very last pannier of Lewis Gun cartridges, his helmet stopped a sniper's bullet and the impact pitched him clean over. The bullet had struck his helmet dead centre, where his forehead was. Leaving a big dent, the shot *skidded* sideways for a good inch. It then *entered the helmet* and fell hot but harmless on Baldwin's bare head. I saw many freak antics by missiles in the course of the war but never anything so peculiar as this. Those among us with a religious turn of mind had their own opinions about such "miracles", but the majority just observed that Baldwin was "bloody lucky" and left it at that.

Of the 200 or so of us who had entered the fort the previous morning, only a grievously depleted remnant had by now survived the 24-hour fusillade. But all Lewis Gun posts remained manned, if depleted, even though they could not continue to operate all out as they might have done – if panniers of bullets had not been left behind at Hinges.

Although our present plight hardly excited any enthusiasm on our part for the unknown designer of our improvised stronghold, it was certainly chosen with an eye to its strategic position command over the roads, or what remained of them, that would serve an enemy's advance on us. Nevertheless, it is doubtful if those planners foresaw anything like the following turn up for the book (from the defence point of view).

Barely a quarter of a mile ahead from our vantage point, a fairly packed column of horse drawn transport, drivers astride their horses as confidently as though they were on a ceremonial parade ground, loomed into our astonished view. They rolled down the road as though they had never heard of a war, and were evidently quite unaware of their dreadful exposure. The German Intelligence Service were evidently worse than useless. Our six Lewis Guns blazed away on the instant, without waiting for any word of command. Those manning the enemy transport, who were not shot down immediately, lashed their horses into a gallop. But our guns soon got their leaders and the whole column piled up in awful, writhing disarray. We ourselves were not without reactions of horror by the frightful havoc we had caused, which was near enough for us plainly to see. This affair as good as finished out Lewis Gun ammunition and we were now defenceless except for a very few cartridges held by those of us who had rifles and revolvers.

Our massacre of the transport was of course the signal for a further frenzied dispatch of lethal hardware by the Germans assigned the job of pulverizing our obstinate fort. Not the least of our predicaments had become the lavatory problem. What make-do receptacles that lay around had already been filled by some previous occupants (Portuguese, we later learned) and although we were fairly immersed in mucky debris no one had the slightest thought of relieving himself on the spot. And so it transpired that little Jack Jones, formerly a Welsh miner, was caught literally with his trousers down, *outside* our fort. A German officer, probably astonished by this bit of British brazenry, and with a distorted sense of humour, began aiming revolver shots at the stooping Jack Jones. The alarmed Jack, clutching his drooping pants, scuttled as hurriedly as he could for any shelter, the German meanwhile following and shooting, but missing. Our Lewis Guns would have put a quick end to this one-sided act had we some ammunition left. As it was, one of our side with a pistol had a go at the German. But all parties survived. The wizardry in shooting accuracy by the cowboys we see in Western films did not exist in the warfare that came my way.

At about 10 a.m. the enemy battering again suddenly ceased, this time for the purpose of allowing a German officer to shout a demand that we surrender.

Speaking in English, he said, "We give you two minutes to come out. If you not come, we blow you all up. You have no chance. We are all around you. Come out, and keep your lives."

"Give us half-an-hour, mate" shouted back one of our fellows. The German might have thought it an accomodating kind of answer but a better understanding of the idiosyncrasy of the English would have shown it up for the derisive and leg-pulling sally it was meant to be.

In any case it was the only answer that could be regarded by the Germans as in any way civil. All the other responses were insulting and scurrilous, most of them being a defiant epithet much more vulgar than "Nuts".

Not surprisingly, the German reaction was a further *strafe,* a very violent one which caused further carnage. In a further half-an-hour all went suddenly quiet again, this time for the same German officer to shout –

"I ask now for the English commanding officer to come out to me. I will show him the position you are in. We do not want to kill any more of you."

A short time elapsed and then I saw our Major, the Officer Commanding, leave our position and go towards the German voice. He looked haggard and pale. So would I have looked in his place.

Our commander returned a little later quite unharmed, rather to the surprise of some of us. He had been shown the formidable array of German guns and general weapons around our fort, all poised to demolish us should we refuse to surrender.

"Our position is now quite hopeless," our Major explained to us, "even if we had ammunition and food. I must now *order* you to surrender."

His order was received with angry imprecations and yells of defiance. It was the one and only occasion I have ever heard British soldiers directly voice disobedience and insubordination to their officer's command. Yet, incredibly enough on this occasion, that officer's order and action saved the lives of most of us, probably all of us.

"I cannot allow you to be killed needlessly," pleaded our Major. "Although surrounded for 30 hours you have held on. I repeat my command that you surrender. It is my duty."

What remained of our sergeants and n.c.o.'s now took it upon themselves to bring home to our men the hopelessness of things and persuade them to give in. And the truculence began to cool down.

Slowly, sullenly and abjectly accepting the position, our chaps began making their guns and other weapons useless to the Germans. As Lewis Gunners we had a machine-gun symbol in the form of a chevron sewn to our shoulder sleeves. Having swallowed the tales that the Germans were now crucifying machine-gunners (a foul falsehood) we tore off those insignias and tried to rub out the traces thereof. But the unfaded patch of clothing where the symbol had been only made the removal the more obvious.

We now slowly left our positions and hesitatingly made our way towards the Germans who now occupied our surroundings in obvious mass. Our exit lay through the old farm yard and then through an archway to the road, where enemy gunners in much force were poised ready for action against any suspicious movement on our part. The few Portuguese who were with us were the first through that archway on the way to give themselves up and get it all over and done with. As I have explained, the British destroyed and abandoned their rifles but the Portuguese retained theirs. They approached the Germans with the rifle bolts drawn back – apparently their token of surrender. Unhappily the Germans either did not understand that gesture or, perhaps more probably, they were taking no chances (this was a period of shooting first and asking afterwards). The Germans let go with machine guns, hand grenades and stick bombs point blank into the concentration of defenceless men in that archway. It was one of the most dreadful massacres it has been my misfortune to see.

Now convinced that the Germans intended a ruthless slaughter, we survivors bolted back from the archway and scrambled among the debris in the farmyard for anything which might serve as weapons. Almost instinctively and without any spoken direction the chaps formed a kind of defensive block. Although of course tense and scared, they were defiantly purposeful, determined to leave this life with as much embarrassment and damage to their assailants as was possible in the desperate circumstances. Yet even in this grim *impasse* there emerged banter and ironic humour. One specimen of encouraging nonsense was when a gaunt, lanky Cockney named Oakley had picked up a pair of tattered and muddy civilian gloves, once yellow. Assuming a post haughtily erect, head arrogantly thrown back, and smoothing those filthy gloves down over his hands in an immaculate Beau Brummel gesture, Oakley languidly drawled:

"Now *do* show a front, C Company. Show the bastards we're British."

His reward was a genuine, albeit weak, smile on many a wan, begrimed face.

IX

SURRENDER

At the command of an enemy officer, the Germans held their fire and the only explosives menacing us were from British artillery. We could only await developments which at length took the form of our own Commanding Officer urging us to go through that arch again. The German commander had now guaranteed our safe transit and, according to our Major, had even apologized for the recent unexpected assault. A resigned, come-what-may demeanour had by now come over most of us, and our officer's persuasion was successful. We began a slow trek towards the Germans. I shuffled out alongside my friend, Ben Toombs (my future brother-in-law, as events turned out). In that accursed archway, one of our men, groaning and bleeding from grenade wounds received during the recent one-sided fracas, was almost prostrate. Lifting him unsteadily to his feet, Ben and I each lent him a supporting arm and the three of us stumbled through the archway to the road outside – and what? Our outside arms were raised, or rather half raised, in token of surrender. The vicinity of the exit was alive with German troops, all at the ready with machine guns, rifles and grenades in case we got fresh.

I was then almost immediately made aware of a revolver held at my belly by a German officer who, with his steel helmet and grim visage, certainly fulfilled the menacing prospect caricatured by our propagandists. This, I instantly made up my mind, was at last *it*. But the privations, ordeals and exhaustion of the past few days had sapped my normal emotions of fear to the extent that my only reaction was a resigned expectation of a bullet in my guts and even a feeling of impatience at the hanging-it-out tactics on the part of my German persecutor.

"Why you not come?" he growled – an allusion to our refusal to surrender long ago.

"Much kamerad dead because you not come," he added. "English good soldat. But no. . . ." For want of a word he tapped his forehead to imply that the English were lunatics.

44

"Answer. WHY?" the officer demanded, meanwhile slightly prodding me with his pistol now and again.

For answer I wearily shrugged my shoulders; and meanwhile I acutely remember observing that the revolver he was brandishing seemed absurdly small in relation to the havoc it was about to cause me. But he did not use it.

"Ugh ... so," he expleted. And my dispirited senses noted, with mild surprise, that he had withdrawn his revolver from my stomach and had turned his attention to the wounded fellow I was still supporting with my right arm. This seemed to be about all the poor chap could take and he looked as if he had about reached the end of his term. The German officer, seeing his desperate condition, turned to me again and said –

"Take your kamerad to that house," That "house" was the pitted three walls remaining of a shell-gutted homestead which the Germans had just improvised as a dressing station for their wounded. It was full of injured German soldiers but my maimed and bleeding British charge was accepted gently and almost amicably by the German orderly looking after the outfit, just as if the business of caring for enemy wounded was a come-day-go-day affair. I began to wonder whether the main difference between British and German soldiers was one of uniform. How could it be that half an hour previously we were doing our utmost to dismember each other's bodies and now they were doing their utmost to patch them up? I have since read that ants do the same thing, after two or more colonies have had a deadly internecine rumpus they will succour and patch up all the ants not dead.

Surprised that I remained alive so far – the German officer who so fiercely interrogated me was after all a humane soldier just doing his job – I then found myself herded among a batch of other British prisoners. We all had to stand by a roadside until our captors organized some guards to convey us away. Meanwhile the British artillery, or what of it that had not been over-run, increased its attention to our immediate locality. Some heavy calibre shells pitched only a few yards away from us and if they had not fallen into soft, recently dug earth, the remnants of our company would have been further reduced. As it happened, the explosives spewed great dollops of muddy clay and loam over us. Although the German soldiery were also at the receiving end of this discomfort, they made known by gesture their sardonic satisfaction at the irony of our being plastered by our own shells.

After a time we were moved on our way by German guards

who expedited our movements with much bayonet brandishing. In common with the general run of recently captured prisoners we looked a sorry, dishevelled and dejected rabble – the kind of spectacle that modern conquerors like to photograph as soon as they can and so present a picture of their enemy's pitiful morale. After shuffling a few hundred yards we could make out some commotion and what seemed to be some violence going on at the head of our column.*

In a field to our right, some German troops were assembling and emplacing a few machine guns.

"Och, this is as far as we go," said a Scots soldier at my side, and the way we prisoners were being marshalled within what looked like the directional sweep of these guns did indeed lend weight to the sinister implication of that Scotsman's utterance. However, after what sounded like an argument between our guards and the gunners we shambled slowly on. But now the continued scuffling up front now revealed its cause. We were being led past the actual spot on the road where we had machine gunned the German transport with the devastating effect I have earlier described. I will not dwell upon the horror of the scene at close quarters except to say that dead horses were sprawled in grotesque attitudes mixed up with the bodies of their late German drivers. As each of us prisoners hobbled past the scene, the German survivors of that transport party be-laboured us with rifle butts or anything else which could hurt. If two of our guards had not rushed up shouting "Halt" and commanding our attackers to ease up we should have been laid out, of that I am sure. So with shaking fists and other menaces, these aggrieved Fritzes let us go with obvious reluctance and a vicious kick at our backsides as each of us filed single past them as quickly as we could. Our guards then continued to lead, or rather drive, us across the shell-tortured terrain.

Our way, to wherever we were being taken, led over our late front line trenches. These British lines had taken a smashing of incredible ferocity. Devastations by bombardment were nothing new to us front line veterans, but here we saw a new High in

* The Battle of the Lys was the last major German offensive against the British on the Western Front. It failed. It wore itself out; a *Misserfolg* to use the Germans' own description of it. In terms of land area however, it made gains which at the time were regarded as enormous and sufficiently perturbed the British High Command to cause Lord Haig's famous Backs to the Wall Order. This was, perhaps justifiably, hailed by the Germans as an announcement betraying panic by the normally phlegmatic English.

fury. Men occupying these trenches could have remained alive only by a miracle.

Awaiting removal to dressing stations, a number of enemy wounded had been collected and placed in dugouts in what had recently been German reserve trenches. It was to be the prisoners' job to carry these wounded to the dressing stations. But the Germans had no proper stretchers available. Instead they intended to make do with trench duckboards. They made the wounded as comfortable as possible by placing their overcoats between the rough wooden battens of the duckboards and their bodies. The combined weight of a wounded man and the heavy trench duckboard was far too much for only two men with four hands, so four prisoners were assigned to carry each "stretcher" – on their shoulders. Before barely 100 yards were covered over the shelled, torn-up and muddy ground, the sharp rough corners of the duckboards began to cut into our shoulders which soon bled profusely. Although we did not know it, we were to be forced to endure about nine miles of this really tortuous ordeal.

The previous sleepless nights, no food for two days, and the strain of the conflicts were having their inevitable effects, and the prisoners began to wilt and then actually collapse under the weight of their burdens and the prolongation of the general sufferings. The German guards were naturally more concerned about the malaise of their wounded comrades than the plight of their British prisoners. So whenever one of the latter showed signs of immobility he was "persuaded" to get going by rifle jabs and threats of more violent action. "Lós . . . lós . . ." incessantly growled these German guards as they prodded the bedraggled column on its faltering way, much as herdsmen urge along a straggling drove of cattle with yells of "girrup-p-p . . . g-i-r-r-u-p."

Thirst added its torment. And as no ordinary drinking water was to be had, the prisoners were lapping up ditchwater with their hands on the very few occasions the guards allowed a wayside halt.

At this point, however, I want particularly to stress that these were the only instances of direct physical ill-treatment during our captivity that I suffered or saw inflicted on British prisoners during the nine months I was incarcerated. Not that our conditions were ever proper. On the contrary they were always pretty barbarous, but here I blame the ruling command and seldom the ordinary German soldiers. Between the common uniformed rank and file of German and British there was

47

largely a bond of understanding and even respect; and the more each other had suffered actual fighting conditions, the greater that mutual sympathy.

In the heat of direct battle some cruelty and excesses were certainly perpetrated, and only to be expected. The assault on us by the survivors of the transport team was in that category.

For all that, I must record that the journey carrying the German wounded impinges on my memory as one of the most horrible and painful episodes I have ever suffered. It ended at the French hamlet of Salome la Bassee. Here we captives were crammed into the rather spacious church, already packed almost to capacity with British and Portuguese prisoners taken elsewhere on the front. The church had for long since ceased to function for religious services. Its normal appointments and furniture had been cleared out, leaving only the walls and the stone floor. It was about 9 p.m. when I and my fellow prisoners were dumped therein. Once left to ourselves we simply let ourselves drop, and a jittery sleep overcame us despite the hard, cold floor and a bitterly cold night. We had no blankets, of course, and no overcoats.

Dawn found most of us awake. Hunger, thirst, bleeding shoulders and exposure made a tormenting combination. I heard some altercation going on between a few prisoners and the German guards at the now opened church doors. The prisoners were pointing to their mouths in an appeal to the sentries to find them some food or drink. Much later a field kitchen did appear and some "soup" was ladled out.

Before I describe the "food" upon which we were to survive, truth and some honesty demand some facts. By April 1918 the Germans were nearly starving. The British naval blockade proved to be the most terribly effective weapon in the Allied armoury. I do not think this stark fact has ever been fully realized or appreciated by those on our side. Only we prisoners, and those of us who were never far from the German fighting troops (I never saw Germany as a prisoner) could perhaps measure the full effect of the privations endured by the German active service men who were standing between the enemy and their Fatherland. I hold no brief for them. How could I be expected to, considering the many miseries they caused me? But I assert that the stand made by the German soldiers in the closing period of World War I should, in the circumstances, rank along mankind's roll of heroics.

While the scarcity of food was their most personal hardship, they were also deprived of innumerable necessities. Wheels were fitted with metal springs in the absence of rubber for pneumatic or solid tyres. This seriously slowed up war transport movements on the damaged roads. As it came my lot to have to make many journeys in their heavy trucks in the war area, I learned what that meant.

They had no petrol as we know it. Instead they made do with a semi-volatile solution they called Benzine, but not the benzine we know. Cloth for surgical bandages ran out, necessitating the use of much less serviceable materials such as existing paper and leaves. Anaesthetics disappeared, and limbs were amputated without.

X

A PRISONER'S LOT

In view of what the Germans themselves were doing without, and the list I have given is no more than a scant abbreviation, it requires no imagination to size up what food and other necessities were likely to be spared for prisoners of war. Captives get the worst of it in the best of wars and although I am very much against the unfair charges that have been made against the Germans they have never been historically very generous to any powerless people in their grasp.

We prisoners were hardly troubled with the shortage of rubber, petrol, bandages, paper, soap and general hardware, but food was another and vital matter. Its availability or absence is the most omnipresent element in the outlook of a prisoner.

The "soup" given to us at Salome was my first shocking acquaintance with our future lot in the way of sustenance.

"This is just bloody sand that the cows have widdled on" said a prisoner on first sampling it.

It was some kind of ground maize dumped in hot water. This grain never integrated with the water. In other words it never dissolved. The mixture was agitated in a cooking tank, but almost immediately after the concoction was served the maize sank to the bottom. The result was worse than indigestible. The men called it Sandstorm, a description which deserves full marks for eloquence. A very meagre portion of black bread was our staple diet for a long time. It's composition eluded description because its darkness obscured its ingredients. The Germans themselves were full of forebodings on the subject and they told us that potato flour and unusual beans entered the bread given to them. I am not sure whether or not the bread given to us prisoners was different, but I can say that many of the constituents we dug out would have caused consternation to the production managers of bakers like Hovis. Among the ingredients not in lumps, sawdust was high on the suspected list.

Even this kind of bread was severely rationed. I never saw larger portions than one small rectangular loaf among five prisoners, and top weight appeared to be about a ¼lb of this black bread a day for one prisoner. I knew the rations on occasions to go as low as one loaf between eight men. At this point I must interject that in the case of very young prisoners, the bread ration did not fall below a certain weight. At that time some scandalously juvenile soldiers were being taken prisoner (on both sides) and in fairness to the Germans it must be recorded that they ameliorated their lot as far as they could in the way of bread rations.

As our allotment of bread was the only solid kind of "bite" we had throughout the day it was most scrupulously apportioned. The Germans delivered the loaves whole and left it to the prisoners to divide the portions. This was a ritual as personal and solemn as a primitive religious sacrament. In one *lager* the participants had constructed a crude balance device with which to weigh the portions of bread they had cut. They would then carefully compare each piece to ensure absolute equality. But not content with that approach to Fair Shares one of the men would place a finger on each of the pieces in turn. "For who?" he would loudly ask. (As he was a Scotsman his inquiry sounded to me like "F . . . r-r-r-oo") Then another chap (with his eyes turned away) would yell Smith or Brown or whatever the name of the chosen recipient to be.

Another grim edible for prisoners was *Sauerkraut*, but the variety given to us must not be confused with the traditional recipe. Owing to the Allied stranglehold on imported foodstuffs the Germans naturally fell back on anything they could grow themselves and *Sauerkraut* comprised just one of such eatables. But as there was a grave limit to what they could produce for their own needs it followed, like all the other things, that what was left for the prisoners would in normal times be rejected garbage. There would also be the addition of strange plant growth that would never be considered fit for human eating at all. At any time *Sauerkraut* is a delicacy exclusive to Teutonic tastes as far as I am concerned; and only the urge to remain on our feet forced us to eat the revolting *ersatz* offered to prisoners.

Wartime *Marmalad*, German for jam, was a concoction of crops, quite unknown to Crosse & Blackwell I am sure, in which mangel-wurzels ruled the roost. As for meat, not a morsel of beef, lamb, port, poultry or any of the viands with which we were once familiar ever came our way. But after several weeks a square of horse meat, about as large as a matchbox, was served to us once a week, usually Sunday. It was ravenously greeted. Our perpetual hunger caused us to regard Sunday as Banquet Day, all because of this spot of horse meat.

Towards the end when even this kind of sustenance was becoming scarcer and scarcer, the Germans pressed some evil tasting fish on the menu. Two prisoners among us who had earned their living in fish markets were quite unable to identify the species, but it was definitely something that once swam and was a big creature. When it reached the prisoners it stank appallingly, although I think its natural pong was augmented by some foul smelling preservative that the Germans used.

Following our breakfast of Sandstorm Soup and a portion of blackbread at Salome on the morning of April 11, we were marshalled for searching and interrogation along a street having a few shops that had recently been shelled and smashed. The Germans took a careful look at any of our possessions (we had only our pockets to turn out) but they confiscated nothing except pocket knives or things which could serve as weapons. Like most other Tommies I had found gambling to be some relief from the tedium of Army life, and while I was with the Expeditionary Force in Italy I had an extraordinary run of luck operating a "Crown and Anchor" Board in the Italian cafes used by the troops (before they were out of bounds). Upon returning to France I changed the Liras to Francs which I stuffed between my underpants and my cyclist breeches just before the Germans caught me. Whether or not the Germans would have relieved me of this money, they failed to find it and this cash was to be a godsend to me before my captivity ended.

The searching completed, there came the questioning. The methodical Germans in no way mixed up the two operations. Now one of the ruined shops in front of which we were lined up had obviously sold hats before the shelling had closed the business, and the stocks of various headgear lay sadly among a heap of plaster and debris. A top-hat, rather dented, rested upright and defiant above the pile. While we prisoners stood dejectedly awaiting the questioning inquisition, one of us, a Welshman named Lacey, darted into this shop, put on the top-hat, and quickly resumed his place in the prisoners' line. The German officer doing the quizzing steadily moved along us, and his demeanour was none too gentle. But his face when he confronted the imperturbable Lacey standing stiffly to attention in the battered and grimy high hat made a picture that would have merited preservation in the National Gallery. The German was moved to smile, as we all did, and the episode lightened our ordeal.

The questioning dealt mainly with our trades in civil life. Our army paybooks were carefully scrutinized for the information they occasionally gave in that direction. In my case it happened that upon joining the Cyclist Company I, with a few others, was sent to the Royal Army Ordnance College at Woolwich for six weeks' course on the maintenance of bicycles. This hardly went beyond the best way of mending punctures, replacing spindles and ball bearings, and speedily doing roadside repairs. As I satisfactorily passed the Course it merited the word ARTIFICER being entered as a qualification in my paybook.

"Ah so: Sie sind Mechaniker," exclaimed the German officer on seeing this, and as a result I was immediately told that I would be sent to one of their motor depots in the war area. My impulse was to run after the German officer to explain that the entry ARTIFICER had nothing whatever to do with motor mechanics, but a German guard with rifle and bayonet effectively deterred my approach. Also winkled out from the common herd, and likewise destined for the garages, were about ten other prisoners. They all had far more practical connections with the motor industry than I, however.

A German then appeared with a large pot of green paint and a brush with which he painted the numbers 71 in huge figures on my back. My newly selected compatriots for the garages were also painted with digits, different ones. This numbering ritual had a humiliating effect that had to be experienced to be appreciated. Nothing like being a walking number to cut one down to size!

We were then ordered to *Kom mit* by one single German with rifle and fixed bayonet. This trooper was entrusted with our delivery to the German motor depot, and off we went. Our destination, not that they told us – and we could not have cared less if they had – was Seclin, a town in the war base area of northern France. It was about 10 miles away from Salome and not far from Lille. After some distance along a canal towpath we began to enter hamlets still occupied by French civilians, the same as was happening on the Allied side. But for us, an amazing difference! These civilians were giving us an affectionate reception, and this required extreme courage on their part.

"Hurrah, les Anglais". "Vive l'Angleterre". These repeated acclamations astonished us. The Germans were implacably hostile to any such demonstrations, and the punishments for attempting to fraternize or communicate with Allied prisoners were ruthless and widely known. Despite this, civilian women and men, and especially the elder children, dared to approach us and attempted to pass pathetic little packets containing slices of bread, or perhaps a potato. Our first impressions of what life was like for civilians under enemy occupation soon came. Passing through a village, one of the German military police, a feared and formidable force known by the French as the Green Devils, let loose his ferocious Alsatian dog upon a boy who had managed to pass a packet of something to one of us prisoners. The boy scurried down a byway, but the dog soon caught him, and there followed a violence of shrieks and savage growls terrible to hear. The treatment of the civilians in the occupied areas was indeed ruthless and merciless, and not just propaganda by the Allies.

Apart from all that, the effect on our morale of this warm attitude of the civilians towards us was terrific in its immediate uplift. Our rather shambling, humiliated and dejected gait became sprightly, almost martial. The men whose tunics were loosened and flopping began to button them up, and when passing any inhabited location they whistled the marching ditties of those days.

The mood of the civilians on the German side of the line towards the British was utterly and strangely different from how we had found the general behaviour of the French natives on our side. This apparent phenomenon is no doubt capable of rational explanation. But the fact remains that after four years of living cheek by jowl on the Allied side, the relations between the British soldiers and the French and Belgian civilians were seldom enthusiastic or even cordial. It was a case of having to live with it. On the German side of the line, the occupied people willingly made sacrifices and often suffered death in their efforts to comfort or release British prisoners. This is no high-faluting essay in glorious prose. It was stark fact in my own personal experience. Indeed I owe my extended existence to one of them!

The ten miles from Salome to Seclin took several hours. I think it was an agreeable diversion of duty for our German guard, a reasonable fellow, and he was in no mood to hurry. German soldiers who happened to see us, exchanged bantering but not unfriendly remarks usually in the pidgin French that both sides used, or some of the German words that were similar to those in English.

"*La Guerre fini pour vouz. Gut, eh Tommy.*" This was, with variation, the general and favourite sally.

"Up the Spurs," was another greeting I heard from a passing German trooper, who evidently wanted to air his familiarity with the football-mad English. The game was not so popular in Germany 50 years ago.

54

A weak but welcome April sun came out *en route,* and some of us began to feel more cheerful. Perhaps, after all, we should survive more tolerably than we feared. *La Guerre,* as far as actual fighting was involved, was indeed *finis pour nous* as the Germans had said, and, after the dicing with death we had endured, no normal human being could feel anything but relief at having escaped from it alive . . .

The motor depot at Seclin had already installed a *lager* for working prisoners and there were a good few of them already there. There was no holiday camp welcome about it and the entrances were studded with notices and warnings that left no doubt about the nationality of those running the outfit. The German language, not generally regarded by a foreigner as entirely picturesque, can look positively terrifying according to one's circumstances.

STAMMLAGER FOR KRIEGSGEFANGENEN was one huge notice, signifying a Concentration Camp for prisoners of war.

HOCHGESCHWINDIGHEIT was to me another repellant mouthful. With 5 km. added after that word, it conveyed a warning that any speed exceeding three miles an hour was *verboten.*

The accommodation separated for the prisoners at the Seclin depot was a large apartment that had once been a big office where accountants worked, judging by the large desks which had steeply sloping tops with ledges down below to support heavy books, presumably ledgers. These were the prisoners' beds. Anything less designed for sleep was unimaginable. On the contrary they could have been a blueprint for insomnia. No prisoner undressed even partially, and except for the rags anyone could scrounge, such as remnants of curtain material or bits of sacking, we remained without anything that might serve as blankets. Sanitation, or more precisely the lack of it, very much increased our nightly misery. Our much tried entrails were now violently rejecting the Sandstorm soup, *sauerkraut,* black bread and other dietetic outrages. The discomfort would have been distressing enough had there been some serviceable kind of latrine, but the only receptacle available for the purpose was one bucket the size of a waste paper bin which was already full before the doors were locked at dusk. In the mornings, the guards listened to our complaints with apparent understanding and sympathy and promised to report the facts, which I believe they did. But nothing was ever done, and this was the kind of cynical and heartless treatment for which those Germans in authority must be heavily indicted. And for much more to come.

While on the subject of sanitation, this meant life in the raw during the daytime. For the use of prisoners, the Germans at Seclin had suspended an ordinary telegraph pole over a deep trench, quite exposed and by the side of a path in full use by French civilians on the other side of a wire fence. The loose stomachs I have described would cause about 20 prisoners at a time to seek a sitting on the pole, and the vista from their rear would be indescribably disgusting and humiliating. French women using the pathway would affect indifference, but nothing at the time could convince us that the Germans had not worked the circumstances deliberately. Whether they did, or whether the Germans were less inhibited about these things than the British, is a matter of conjecture.

The work we were having to do for the Germans so far did not go very high up the technical ladder. The prisoners were at first applied to the dirty jobs such as refuse removing, floor washing or loo cleaning. Later on it became much more arduous. From early morning to dusk we were forced to work on the heaviest of tasks and on near-starvation rations. Mixing seemingly endless quantities of cement and moving heavy loads of all kinds, the most trivial refraction would bring punishment. The favourite in this camp was to compel two delinquents to carry a section of ordinary railway line suspended shoulder to shoulder around the compound. Before long one of the "malefactors" would drop under the sheer weight of the iron rail and in any case both would nurse bruised and bleeding shoulders for days to come. Today I read what do-gooders say about punishment being no deterrent. I can only say that the treatment I have described had a salutary effect on would-be infringers. Which is not saying that it was the proper thing to do.

This is where, as with many other failings in their treatment of prisoners, the Germans did not play the game. I am trying to be fair and not to exaggerate my accounts of their behaviour, I have already said that I personally saw them commit no direct physical violence on a prisoner. But they were all more than usually prone to overdo any authority they had over those in their power and they would without question carry out the orders from their superiors however inhumane they might be. That is why I put most of the blame on to the German Top Brass.

The international agreements on prisoners of war, to which

the Germans were signatories, provided that captives should neither be forced to labour in the fighting lines nor to work on munitions of war. We were forced to do both, especially to toil in the fighting areas which, towards the end of the war, were veritable infernos by Allied action. The British, at any rate, did behave in a proper way to all their prisoners. I had some experience which convinced me that there was little doubt about that. On many occasions my Cyclist Company was called upon to act as sentries over sudden concentrations of German prisoners. The food we gave them was equal in quantity and quality with what was given to British soldiers, and the Germans were the first to admit the excellence of these rations compared with what they had been living on before capture. Moreover, the British saw to it that their prisoners were accommodated and clothed in a proper way at the earliest opportunity. A sense of decency demanded that this should be, and it required no authority to dictate it. It was a matter of playing the game.

The German tactics in compelling their prisoners to work recoiled very heavily to their disadvantage in some cases, as I shall narrate.

After a few weeks at Seclin, most of us were transferred to another and bigger German garage and motor repair depot at Roubaix, a large industrial centre in northern France, almost adjoining Lille. Here the large building which the Germans had put to use for this motor depot was a textile factory in pre-war days. A spacious room on the ground floor had been set apart for the *kriegsgefangenen* and there were about 200 of them, all allegedly motor mechanics. Although we prisoners were cheek-by-jowl in our new quarter (it takes a large room to give much elbow room to 200 bodies) the conditions were an improvement on those at Seclin.

The wooden floor was our bed, but most of us in time scrounged something soft to act as a mattress to cushion our bones against the unyielding planks. On the other side of the medal, anything at all eatable became increasingly scarce. Prisoners who had been settled in the German heartland were succoured by monthly food parcels through the Red Cross Society (God bless 'em) but none reached us who had been detained in the war area – for the simple reason that the Germans had so far prevented any news of our survival reaching the Allied Command. This was one more grave and inexcusable cruelty inflicted by our captors, and the charge is proven and quite undeniable.

Despite our daily ration of black bread becoming smaller and smaller, we each tried to divide it into three bites a day. It seemed to space out the incessant gnawings of an empty stomach into more tolerant intervals. As a general rule the bread was issued to us in the evening, which meant that we had to hold it overnight. And *holding* it was a literal necessity. I learnt how little time it takes for hunger to strip from men the thin veneer of civilized culture, and that so many of them will sink to any depravity or take any risks when their bellies are empty. So it was that some of our own fellow prisoners would prowl around the others' sleeping places during the night in the hope that they could steal their frugal morsels. This caused the men to pass the nights sleeping with one eye open so to speak, all vowing absolute murder should they catch anyone in the act — and meaning just that! At infrequent intervals during the night the crash of a heavy wooden clog on the floor boards meant that someone suspected the proximity of one of these marauders and had taken blind aim in the dark with his foot-gear. Quite a few of these episodes were false alarms, but owing to the utter lack of light it was not possible to make sure.

The mention of clogs prompts me to explain that leather was another of the commodities in great shortage with the Germans. They therefore relieved British prisoners of their good leather boots and gave them heavy wooden clogs instead. British soldiers who were left dead in German areas after a battle were always without their boots. We never got used to the clogs and would wrap our feet in rags to lessen the chafing.

The British Royal Flying Corps began night bombing raids and this caused the Germans to black out the windows and smother the faintest glimmer of light. The doors of our *lager* were then bolted and the German guards kept their watch from without.

XI

NON-COOPERATION

At first the day's work for all prisoners was confined to the garages. A constant flow of vehicles, mainly heavy trucks, came in for maintenance and repair. Most of these bore the name Wanderer. There was also a mini-size Wanderer and it was a very ingenious product for those days.

Some prisoners were put on washing and cleaning the various parts that needed attention before those jobs earned the attention of the skilled German mechanics. Prisoners were not allowed to deal with technical components like magnetos or carburettors or bearings. But we could replace sparking plugs or be sent underneath to put split pins in bolts that were in remote, begrimed and uncomfortable positions. In this the Germans simply asked for trouble – and they got it! Sabotage was easily but efficiently organized. Every night after the day's work, there were surreptitious meetings of the prisoners who each gave an account of what damage he had been able to do. They also advanced and compared ideas and ways and means of inflicting the maximum sabotage with the minimum fuss. Some tactics were simplicity itself. For examples we all had pocketsful of old screws, filings and the tiny metallic bits and pieces that strew workshop floors. As prisoners had to sweep the floors it was just no problem at all to collect any amount of such small junk.

Not a sparking plug was replaced by a prisoner unless a few odds and ends like old screws went down the cylinders first. The effect would not show until the vehicle had left and was under way. Then, of course, the metal foreign bodies would become incandescent and cause pre-ignition.

Those of us on our backs underneath lorries would never dream of replacing one split pin without removing two others – and loosening operational nuts elsewhere in the bargain!

Some of our fellow prisoners really were professional motor mechanics in civil life, and many of their antics for shortening the lives of the electrical and other technical components could fill a book on their own. This went on undetected for months. The huge *Wanderer* trucks would be returned to the garages again and again by irate drivers who would often give lively accounts of having conked out and being stuck for hours in heavily shelled areas. Incidentally I could appreciate the point of view of these drivers because Nemesis overtook me on one occasion. I was sent out on a working job in one of the actual lorries we had treated. It shuddered to its stoppage right on an exposed and shelled crossroad near Armentières where we were marooned all night.

When a German mechanic was thought to be negligent or inefficient, his punishment was transfer to the infantry or to one of the other fighting Units. This was a dreaded prospect and a perpetual nightmare to those it might affect. Although in my experience the average German male made a good and formidable soldier when events demanded it, he was less inclined to romantic heroics about it than most other European subjects. In other words he found nothing noble about being sent to the trenches.

It did happen several times that German mechanics were unjustly removed from the garages as a result of our sabotages, and I must record that it weighed very heavily on our consciences. So much so that prisoners who had caused the particular damage would sometimes be on the point of confessing involvement and so save a German mechanic, whom they had grown to like, from being unfairly accused and sent to the trenches. In the final, rather painful, analysis, however, there was always the consolation that we might be saving the lives of our compatriots on the other side.

Reflecting upon the prejudices and acrimony that naturally and inevitably cause rows among any normal community of any 250 *well fed* and affluent human beings, it requires no great imagination to realize the squabbles, bad tempers and eventual hatreds which stewed in one concentration of 250 men cooped up in one big room and cut off from all normal amenities, unwashed, lousy and near starving. Very often in such circumstances a petty incident magnified itself until it provoked agitations out of all proportion to its justice or importance. One such niggling bone of contention was whether our non-commissioned officer prisoners, sergeants corporals, etc., should continue to have authority over us now that we were all prisoners. The trouble boiled up mostly because the sergeants would make it their responsibility to parade us all outside the *lager* every morning and midday, in the rather peremptory manner they had been used to, then report to the German commandant that we were all duly assembled, and afterwards march us off to work. That done, the N.C.O.'s would return to their quarters, since they were not forced to work by the Germans.

This grievance, well fermented for weeks by a few of the more vociferous among the prisoners, finally found violent expression one morning in June. A terrace, in the form of an embankment, ran immediately outside the length of our prison, and it was some 15ft higher than the terrain below which it joined by way of a grassy incline.

One Sergeant Harris had formed us up along this embankment and while he waited to report that fact to our German masters he found himself the target of some outspoken and abusive epithets on the subject of toadying to the enemy.

"What a bloody arse-crawler!" sneered someone in the line.

"We'll show him when this bloody lot's over" threatened another.

The sergeant approached face to face with the man who had made the last remark.

"Was that you said that?" asked he.

The sergeant threatened dire consequences. He would tell the German commandant. Thereupon a Private Peebles, formerly of Glasgow, hit the sergeant full in the face and followed it with a vicious head-butt. The blows rolled the sergeant down the grassy embankment. The Germans punished Peebles with a period of solitary confinement, on half rations which at that time meant almost nothing. And this incident had consequences which involved me. The German commandant in charge of this establishment, which included the motor depot as well as the prison camp, was an officer named Imhof. He was the embodiment of all we thought to be typical of the German military Top Brass, both to look at and to listen to. But, in retrospect, taking him all round, he wasn't a bad chap. He had a lot to put up with, and at times tolerated moves by me which he need not have done.

As a result of the battering suffered by the sergeant he caused the removal of all our non-commissioned officers. The incident really did them a good turn because they were sent to an established prison camp inside Germany which, while no Butlin's, was a holiday resort compared with our concentrations behind the lines.

Imhof insisted, however, that one among the ordinary prisoners remaining should be deputed to "run" the camp and be responsible to the Commandant; and that the prisoners themselves should elect that candidate for this onerous, invidious and unpaid office.

I was the only prisoner in the camp who could apparently manage any kind of connected intercourse in German, however elementary. Probably because of that I was chosen by my fellow captives to officiate in the way the Commander Imhof had in mind. Not surprisingly I tried to wriggle away from this dubious honour, but it was one of those crucial junctures where normally nondescript beings have Greatness thrust upon them. My relations with Imhof soon assumed a constant kind of feud because of the perpetual complaints I had to bring to him on behalf of the prisoners. For all that he never did me a bad turn when he could often have done so.

The end of June arrived and we had been prisoners for three months. Yet we had not been given facilities to write home and there was not the slightest sign of such. We afterwards learned that our existence as prisoners had never been officially notified by the Germans. After some weeks the British authorities had therefore officially reported us "missing, believed dead" to our next-of-kin. When, after a few further weeks had gone by, and there was still no report by the Germans, the British War Office informed our families that it must regretfully be assumed that we were killed in action. In my case a touching letter was sent to my parents by a padre with the glorious consolation that I was fighting bravely when last seen – a stereotyped figment of official imagination . . .

One of my first efforts as spokesman was to get something done about some means of communication with our relatives at home. I nagged away at Imhof every time I saw him, which was at least twice daily. When I was able to bring home to him the barbarity of the circumstances he did express understanding and said he would press his superior command for the necessary arrangements. I was satisfied that Imhof kept his promise, but the German Chief of Staff to whom he was subservient ignored his communications and altogether showed a cynical indifference to the matter. The reason, I think, was pretty obvious. The Germans were detaining us in the fighting zones as a labour force, doing what direct combatants would otherwise do, in perilous and revolting conditions that no stretch of imagination could call camps; and rather than divulge that offence against international war law they preferred our people to infer that we were missing and dead.

The iniquity of the position became an obsession with us and at one of our "bush telegraph" meetings we resolved on some kind of direct and obvious protest, whatever the risk. So one night it was agreed unanimously by the whole camp that all the prisoners would refuse the order to move off to work the following morning.

Since the sergeant was knocked down by Peebles, and removed, it became my job to marshall the fellows on the embankment outside the prison every morning. They themselves asked me to act in that capacity because they preferred to have me doing it than a German. This done it was the daily habit of a German sergeant to yell *Rechts um*, at which command the men would Right Turn and await his further order to march away to their various places of work.

"*Rechts um*," rasped the German officer on the critical morning.

No one moved.

"*Was ist lös!*" roared the astonished German at this strange, unprecedented and flagrant disobedience.

"*Rechts um*," he literally screamed, once again.

Not a move.

"Tookeer" (how the Germans pronounced my name, Tucker) "*was is den lös?*" What's going on?

I then explained (as was pre-arranged with our fellows) that this was the prisoners' protest at the German refusal to make facilities for writing to their parents or at least to make known to them that they were still alive, although captured.

"*Ah, so*" observed the officer, with a steely glare.

He strutted to the extreme right-hand man of the line of prisoners, fixed him with a grim stare for a second or two, positioned his revolver about an inch from his throat, and simply growled "*Rechts um*", his finger ominously on the trigger.

After about ten seconds, but what seemed to me a good ten minutes, our involved prisoner sullenly but obediently turned right. The German then subjected the next prisoner in line to the same operation. He turned in five seconds The next turned immediately and the remainder turned without further command.

Had his order been downright disobeyed I have no doubt that the officer would have used his gun. His reaction was certainly effective, and on the face of it the protest was a humiliating fizzle. But it wasn't! The incident provided me with material for a written report which Imhof, to his credit, passed to his Headquarters. Within a week, two sentries (with fixed bayonets, I don't know why) came to the camp asking for "Tookeer" and I was formally marched outside the factory and across the road to the Commandant's office. Imhof then explained to me that an address had been arranged for us. The address was the Kriegs-gefangenen Lager at Friedrichsfeld bei Wesel. This Friedrichs-feld was hundreds of miles from us, well into Germany. None of us ever saw it, or any other place in Germany for that matter. However, the Germans arranged that correspondence for us would be redirected to where we were, and by that means they would be able to cloak the place where they were actually keeping us. However, I had the great pleasure of distributing two official postcards to each of my fellow prisoners upon which they hastened to communicate the news of their survival to their dear ones in Britain, about four months after their capture.

XII

RELAXATION

The Germans were at all times opposed to any fraternization between the occupied civilian population and the prisoners of war. Any attempts at communication were ruthlessly suppressed by penalties such as confiscation of property, prison, deportation, and often death. In spite of these deterrents, the civilians were always on the watch for some means of easing our lot. Their favourite and safest way as a rule was to offer various things through their local mayor or mayoress (usually the mayoress because her husband was unavoidably absent). Among the few other offerings that the prison commandant allowed the mayoress of Roubaix to give us was a piano, and this turned out to be a very welcome acquisition. Around its presence there developed organized concert parties, crude comedies, almost sophisticated plays, and the usual run of musical entertainments. An incredible flow of latent theatrical talent oozed from the prisoners. The fact that "props" were hard to come by, and rather rough when they did come, only served the more to invoke masterpieces of ingenuity in adapting the makeshift material to the purpose in view. Charles Dickens himself would have been intrigued could he have attended the prisoners' performance of *Oliver Twist*. The absence of any Board of Censors allowed his famous characters to indulge in licentious acts and utterances that rather strayed from the original, but the result was equally entertaining. I became well involved with the nightly musical sing-alongs and "productions", because I could play the piano – after a style.

The Germans, too, had their own (mistaken) ideas on what we might consider "entertainment". This took the form of compulsory attendance (for which they charged the 10 pfennigs which by international agreement they paid us each week for working) at some film shows heavily and artlessly loaded with propaganda. One spectacular they were fond of showing us again and again was an array of British battleships left damaged and half sunk by the Mole at Zeebrugge, after the epic British naval raid on the German submarine base there. The German film naturally did not explain that the very presence of the shattered and submerged British warships was the sole object of the attack, namely to sink the vessels in the narrow channel at the harbour entrance and thus block the freeway at this important submarine base.

These film shows were invariably received by the prisoners with noisy derision. One show in particular was very noisy. The prisoners had all been herded to their seats, but something prevented the German pianist from turning up and his absence was delaying the performance. A German officer, announcing this, asked if there was present a British prisoner who could play the piano and who would volunteer to substitute for the German instrumentalist. I did *not* volunteer. But I was bodily hustled to the piano by some of my fellow prisoners who, in the circumstances, had very quickly assessed the opportunity of expressing their sentiments in a way quite contrary to what the Germans had in mind.

Frankly ill at ease and fidgetting on the piano stool I hammered out a few bars as "overture". The picture began. But as the piano was placed at the extreme edge of the picture sheet, and in line below it, I could not see it and had no idea of what was being shown. I could not therefore choose music appropriate to the film – even had I wanted to.

The showing had hardly got under way when one of our fellows edged near me saying quietly but rather excitedly:

"Bill. Play *Fred Karno's Army.* Now."

This was a current barrack-room lament.

Now it happened that the Kaiser was at that time doing a series of morale-raising visits to some of his hard pressed troops in northern France. What was showing while I was playing was a film high-lighting His Imperial Highness receiving the March Pasts etc. etc., all in the spectacular goose stepping and pompous ceremonial fashion of German military tradition. However, I played what I was asked. Whereupon the prisoner audience very gustily sang, to the tune of a well-known hymn: –

We are Fred Karno's Amy, the Kaiser's Infantry,
We cannot shoot, we cannot fight, what bloody good are we,
And when the English win the war, the Kaiser he will say,
Hoch Hoch, Mein Gott, what a bleedin' fine lot,
Are the Kaiser's Infantry.
A...M...E...N.

This derisive dirge was loudly repeated for the entire duration

of this particular film sequence and it ended with some boister-
ous hooraying by the prisoners. The German officers and
guards who were there concealed what mystification or ire this
interlude must have caused them. Or maybe the humour and
irony of this typical British demonstration was not understood
by them.

For the next ten minutes or so the pictures were apparently
concerned with domestic or mundane topics, although I still
had no idea because of my "blind" position.

After a short break came a fresh film which immediately
caused some of my compatriots to croak the first melodic lines
of the patriotic Victorian music hall number "Sons of the Sea:
all British boys. . . ."

This was their cue for me to play it. The prisoners immediately began a full throat rendering of this bellicose
ballad. . . .

"They may build their ships my lads,
And think they know the game,
But they can't beat the boys of the Bulldog Breed,
That made old England's name. . . ."

and at this point a violent swipe removed me from the piano.

The picture had been a German documentary purporting to
show the havoc being wreaked on British ships by the U Boats.
The German submarines did of course inflict tremendous
damage on the Allied effort, but this film absurdly exaggerated
the position and was vainglorious in most aspects. In any case it
failed entirely and ignominiously to impress its prisoner
"audience"; each bombastic achievement was greeted with
stampings on the floor and defiant imprecations.

We were not invited to any more film shows.

July 1918. For the three months we had now been in enemy
hands the racket and rumble of artillery fire, so familiar to us
every day for the preceding three or four years, had been notice-
ably absent. Held, as we were, so near to the original front, this
silence was a melancholy and nagging reminder to us that the
British must have suffered a heavy blow which had forced them
back to a distance too far for the noise of gun duels to reach
us.

Had anyone told us six months ago that the rumble of guns
would have fallen on our ears like a harmonic and delightful
concerto we should have told him to have his head seen to. But
such did come to pass when one morning our ears joyfully
received the unmistakable cannonade of an artillery barrage. So

the Allies had pushed up nearer to us than our captors had led us to believe – indeed, had we taken much notice of their tales we should have believed that the Germans were already in the Channel Ports preparing to occupy England. Anyhow, we now knew that the British were still a fighting force, whether they or the Germans were doing that firing, and the realization enthused in us an uplift almost beyond description.

From every aspect the shortage of German manpower, and the deterioration in the quality of it, was now becoming very evident. The same could be said about the British plight, judging by the extremely juvenile appearance and inexperience of the latest prisoner-of-war-arrivals.

The Germans were throwing into their fighting line every man who was capable of movement. They therefore began using those prisoners like us whom they held in the war area, just behind the trenches, on labours which were normally the work of combatant troops. These were tasks such as ammunition moving, repairing and maintaining shelled roads, and any heavy and unpleasant jobs that were around.

On many of these working parties they would make me accompany the squads of my fellow prisoners for the purpose of interpreting the orders. This role went very much against my grain, but our own chaps urged me to do it because they would suffer far more discomfiture if a German took my place.

A German army motor truck would be sent to the depot for about 12 prisoners. The driver and his mate, armed with revolvers, would take us to the jobs. The same Germans came on several occasions. They were decent fellows, just doing what they had to, and after a time we were all tolerably friendly together. The driver told me his name was Paul. So what more harmoniously apposite than to hitch the nickname Peter to his mate?

Some filthy assignments came our way on these working parties. One particularly revolting one was to disengage a dead and putrifying horse from the wheels and chassis of a heavy motor truck. A shell had killed the horse. The lorry had crashed into and over it and swerved into a deep ditch. After heaving backwards, forwards, sideways, as well as lifting and tugging, we raked and scooped the motor truck clear of the clinging and nauseating carcass of the unfortunate horse. This rather long operation was complicated by some persistent shelling by the British who, having spotted our activity did their best to annihilate us, not dreaming on British prisoners working so near the line.

Peter and Paul then hitched a tow rope from their truck to the vehicle in the ditch with the intention of pulling the latter out on to the road. Instead, the effort caused their own truck to skid sideways and end up with its own wheels down the muddy ditch as well. This bungled manoeuvre effectively blocked the road which was soon jammed and snarled up with German infantry and transport on its way to repel what, judging by the hell beginning to break, was an impending British assault. It was quite beyond our power to extricate the two trucks, a turn of events which gladdened rather than saddened us British prisoners.

But Peter and Paul had become really desperate. To my astonishment they asked me to go alone to a fair size building, which they pointed out to me, about a third of a mile away. I was to ask there for the German lieutenant, request him to send back with me six of his men, and tell him why. Setting off on the way, I was soon mixed up with moving batches of German soldiery, field guns, limbers, and the general paraphernalia of troops approaching a battle zone, and a lively one at that.

The fantastic circumstances of the moment gradually dawned on me. Here was I, a lone prisoner-of-war, free in a way for the first time for months, yet mingling kind of legitimately with enemy soldiers. I was still wearing my British khaki tunic and breeches, but they were under an old suit of blue overalls which I had scrounged from one of the French civilians who worked in the Roubaix motor depot. I also wore a civilian cap which had seen better days. But although I could have been the only "civilian" in that area so near the front the abnormality was either lost on the German troops, or they cared not. Escape? The possibility reared automatically in my imagination. Escape was never far from our thoughts, whatever the circumstances. I weighed up the prospects as I trudged towards that building. But the outlook was hopeless, and I knew it. Although the thunderous inferno seemed to be in the direction I was heading, the front was seldom a straight line for long but rather a tortuous series of salients, twists, sapheads, redoubts and barbed wire. Escapes were only probable away from the lines, not through them. I could never reach the British trenches via the German trenches in one piece, and I confess that I did not take long to abandon that idea. So I arrived at that building.

The British were now doing some saturation shelling. A number of tight lipped, apprehensive German warriors were crouched around the building, all harnessed with full equipment and weapons, obviously awaiting trouble. Approaching one of them I asked:

"Is your Lieutenant here?"

My un-native rendering of German caused him to stare at me for longer than I thought comfortable, before he replied:

"What did you say?"

I repeated my question.

"You are not a German," he asserted.

"No. I am an English prisoner-of-war," I replied.

"*Ein Tommy?*" he inquired, obviously startled.

"*Hey, Hey,*" he shouted to his comrades. "*Hier ist ein Tommy.*"

A few of them joined the party and one of them turned back the edge of my old blue overall, exposing my British army khaki tunic.

"*Yah, ein Tommy,*" they almost gasped, one after the other.

The atmosphere was not all that cordial. So once more I asked:

"Is your Lieutenant here? It is important."

One of them did say:

"*Yah, yah. Hier bleiben ein moment.*"

And so that I did *bleib*, one of his friends grasped my wrist.

Duly in *ein moment* a German officer did show up. He knew a smattering of English, and I thought it circumspect to let him call most of the tune in the choice of language.

"You, *ein Tommy, hein?*" he asked suspiciously and somewhat threateningly, eyeing my now exposed uniform.

"*Warum* you here, eh?"

Interrupting my efforts to explain, he continued:

"What think you of your *kameraden* now?"

At that precise moment my *kameraden* were cannonading the building and its precincts with just about everything explosive that was known to warfare. A king-size (probably 15in.) projectile screamed its arrival. Two of the German soldiers around, just boys, whimpered audibly in a way I knew so well to indicate simple panic.

"Eh Tommy" the officer added. "Love you your *kameraden* now?"

For answer I weakly shrugged my shoulders. "It is war," I said in the absence of anything more sensible to give in reply to a senseless question.

My British comrades then emphasized their proximity by blowing the remaining roof tiles all over us. I was by now feeling decidedly uneasy. In situations like this, human nature is not at its most benevolent. Here was I, a suspicious looking and defenceless representative of the enemy who was causing all this trouble. What more reasonable than to expect at least a clout from one of these alarmed and rugged soldiery surrounding me? But:

"*Yah, yah: es ist krieg,*" was the officer's fully agreeable reply. He merely added: "What want you?"

I explained how my German guard had sent me to him with the request for at least six of his men to help extricate the trucks from the ditch. He at once detailed seven; and there followed the strange procession of one unkempt English prisoner leading seven heavily armed German soldiers back to where I came from. They accompanied me obediently along the war strewn and bombarded tracks, and I seemed to be the only one who saw anything odd about the mix-up. I am sure no German prisoner ever led seven British soldiers along in similar circumstances.

The seven Germans and the six British prisoners finally heaved the lorries from the ditch – rather to the disappointment of the captives whose main satisfaction in life these days was in causing or watching impediments to the German war effort.

XIII

THE PETTICOAT LINE

By now our deteriorated state of personal hygiene can only be described as revolting. There was nothing in the way of organized baths and although we did what we could, and as often as possible, with the uncertain availability of water and the crude receptacles that we found around, it was more often than not impossible to have more than a cat-lick.

I had now worn for more than five months the same set of underwear. While it is true that every soldier on the Western Front was probably lousy, the periodical changes of underclothes, and the frequent roastings by candlepower along the seams of our tunics (especially around the neck), did help to inflict some reduction of our loathsome parasites. But in our conditions as prisoners, the infestation raged unchecked and naturally the result was diseases. Considering our proximity to their own servicemen, working with them as we were, it astonished me that the Germans did not pay more attention to the problem if only for their own sakes.

Anyway, now that I was kind of shop steward for the prisoners, the question of some change of underclothes was continually a barbed topic between me and the Commandant who always replied that it was now difficult to give even their own men a change of underwear. This was indeed true, so desperately disorganized and short of necessities had the Germans become. So I was the more elated when one day the Commandant told me that he had been able to make some arrangements with the local French civilian laundry for some supply of undergarments for the prisoners, on an exchange basis.

Accordingly, one morning a German sentry, complete with his ubiquitous rifle with fixed bayonet, duly called at the depot for me and escorted me along to this laundry. A small army of French women worked the establishment under the supervision of an elderly looking soldier of the German *Landstürmer* – a kind of Home Guard. This chap, an affable old boy, had been told I would be coming.

"Kom mit, Tommy" said he. He led me to a huge washing room and pointed to nine army-type shirts lying on the floor.

"Pour vous," he said (the Germans often used simple French, just as we did on our side) with a flourish that implied unbounded generosity.

"But there are 250 of us" I cried. "What good are nine shirts among all those?"

"Das its ALLES" he answered with definite finality, brandishing a form of receipt for nine shirts for me to sign.

By now a number of the French washing girls had gathered around us, attracted by the unusual accents of their visitor. They had evidently never been so near a real British soldier before (assuming that a prisoner of war in some sartorial disarray could pass for the real thing).

"C'est un Anglais?" asked one of the ladies.

"Yah. Er ist ein Tommy," replied the old *Landstürmer*

This let loose a necking assault that smothered me. It made absolutely no difference that they were dealing with a dishevelled, half-starved travesty of the dashing British army. It was enough that I was a British Tommy and for that they all gave me a passionate hug.

Two or three of the girls made gestures unmistakably symbolic of sexual goings on. One of them, somewhat more practical than the others, actually prostrated herself on my pile of nine shirts in willing expectation. *"Yah, yah; gut, gut!"* repeatedly urged the amiable old *Landstürmer,* and as evidence of his whole-hearted cooperation he offered me his bunch of keys in case I might want to lock the door against nosey intruders. Alas for the cause of romance, however, the male partner for this proposed rapture was at the moment no more physically or mentally able to go through with it than he could have galloped up Everest. Although several years of war service had certainly lessened some inhibitions, I would have been utterly incapable of becoming a satisfactory paramour in the presence of her many lady friends, in a huge room in broad daylight, and under an enormous skylight.

"I come back later," I said, several times; not wishing to upset the Entente Cordiale. And after a spate of *au revoir* embraces I got outside with my nine shirts. I returned in silence with my guard, excited but strangely wistful as a result of this unexpected episode.

When I rejoined my fellow prisoners I made a pathetic and cheerless job of confessing that I had brought back only nine

73

shirts and that at this weekly rate it would take at least 27 weeks for all 250 of them to have one change. Happily, the usual humour traditional with our chaps seeped through at this juncture and the camp committee (half a dozen of us who unofficially maintained domestic order among the prisoners) decided to raffle the shirts. The fact that I personally "won" a shirt was a silent but eloquent gesture from my comrades that they appreciated my efforts notwithstanding the almost negligible results. I kept very quiet about the laundry girls!

Not being in a recognized or organized prisoners' camp, none of the internationally agreed amenities, however small, were readily available to us. We had to agitate for every single "right". For one thing, prisoners of war who work are entitled to a small regular payment from their captors, but there was no question of our being paid anything until I repeatedly pestered our subjugators. When they did eventually agree to pay us, the amount allowed was 10 pfennigs (in those days less than 1p) a week, and the Germans said I would have to write up the weekly payment sheets for the Roubaix prisoners. So once weekly I had to go to an office in the motor depot, where I would render this mighty epic in accountancy (totalling about £3.00 in present currency) under the eyes of German service soldiers who were the counterpart of our Army Pay Corps.

Contemptuous of the niggardly treatment and not being overtroubled with any qualms about honesty in such circumstances I fiddled the books to a scandalous extent. For one example: I had to make column lists of the names for payment, the surnames first and then the full Christian names in that order. I duplicated and triplicated that order in reverse etc.; e.g. ... BROWN. John Michael: MICHAEL, John Brown: JOHN, Michael Brown. They just paid out the totals I showed, with little or no check, and I applied the surplus to camp use.

In this pay office I became acquainted with Charlot, a noncommissioned officer in the German Army, to whom I shall refer later.

The working parties under the orders of the drivers Peter and Paul continued. Although the tasks to which we were put were nearly always dirty, heavy and in danger from our own guns, the prisoners were always eager to be picked for them. Although they had to travel inside the trucks and therefore could not see much, it was the one and only way of getting away from the dreary confines of the prison compound for a few hours. I was made to go on most of them for liaison between prisoners and guards and it was left to me to choose the fellows who went on these parties. On the way to the jobs I had to sit in the driving cabin between Peter and Paul.

One day the truck was laden with sacks of potatoes which the prisoners were required to hump into the cookhouses of some German service units in the advanced areas. The potato was now the staple and coveted item of diet for the Germans in their now desperate shortage of anything edible.

During this journey Peter and Paul uneasily confided to me that they were up to something rather irregular that day. It would be good for me if I and my comrades were cooperative. As I had no ready answer to this, not having any idea what was afoot, Peter and Paul regarded my silence as a token of agreement. Not long afterwards they drove the truck to a remotely situated French café-estaminet which they reached by a back road then so little used that its cobbled surface was overgrown with grass and weeds.

"Tommy. Tell your comrades to unload six sacks. Quickly," said Peter to me in German. I duly conveyed the order to my friends, who promptly did as requested.

This meant that Peter and Paul were robbing the German Army of their precious potatoes and selling them to the *patronne* of this French café, a formidable looking female of gnarled visage. She seemed indeed the type that ran one of the underworld vice joints which thrived close to the fronts of both sides.

While the lady was handing over payment in the form of a fat wad of Mark notes, Paul told her that I was a Tommy. She had become so jittery, however, that the information did not quite register, and in any case I sure she did not care who I was. Peter and Paul had also become apprehensive, nervy and itching to be off – with sound reason too, since the firing squad was the one and only end to anyone caught at this kind of game. Indeed the lorry was actually pulled up for investigation soon after by German military police in a nearby street; but they assumed that the presence of the British prisoners was ample assurance that nothing could be amiss. The episode gave me a few qualms after the event. Had those military police not been bamboozled, the prisoners in the lorry would surely have been suspected of complicity and, although really innocent, would have suffered dire consequences.

Nearing the end of that journey, Peter and Paul pulled up at another café-restaurant on the outskirts of Roubaix. By then they had regained their breezy composure, but it was undoubtedly well in their minds that I had been a witness to all they had been up to. Either this, or even in some gratitude for my supposed help, they invited me into the café with them for a drink. I agreed to this with pleasure.

It was a very large café, furnished with the usual round tables, and packed full of sitting and standing German soldiers, all with full equipment and rifles. They were obviously having a rest *en route* for the trenches. Peter and Paul sat me down with them at a table at which there were already seated three German troopers. So far they took little notice of me because my old overalls effectively obscured my British khaki tunic.

A young French woman with large, sad, but made-up eyes and flaming red hair – I shall never forget her – took the order for our three drinks. When she returned with the drinks and put them on the table, Paul said casually, "Julie. *Er ist ein Tommy.*"

The young lady eyed me with some indifference.

"*Non Non,*" declared Julie, still looking at me. "*C'est pas possible.*"

For reply, Paul undid and turned aside my overalls, thus exposing my uniform.

Julie stared intently at my khaki tunic for quite a few seconds, then suddenly and without another word she flung herself on me in violent embrace, hurling me back on the table top. All the drinks went flying. The shattering of glasses and general commotion of course attracted the attention of this room full of German soldiery. I had hardly extricated my dishevelled and bewildered self when Julie grasped my wrist and tugged me away.

"*Kom mit,* Tommy," she murmured.

She pulled me through the bar into a bedroom. There she forthwith proceeded with those preparations usually associated with wedding nights, and I could not help thinking that she was not unfamiliar with the process, judging by the speedy and confident way she was handling the circumstances. There could of course have been some cause for haste, remembering that a horde of Germans were languishing in the bar waiting to be served.

But in me I am afraid the lady had not met her Casanova. Not for a moment am I claiming that any moral precepts disturbed me. Oh no! The beasts-in-the-field existence that had been our lot in those years had effectively removed that kind of veneer. But for one thing, the proximity of a squad of enemy soldiers in an adjoining room is hardly an aphrodisiac; for another, a diet of sandstorm and *sauerkraut* is no love potion; and, moreover, the brutal suddenness of this *affaire* were altogether very depressing ingredients for a passionate love episode.

I pleaded the awkwardness of our circumstances to an obstinate Julie who meanwhile persisted in her endeavours to have the liaison consummated adequately to her standards. Suddenly, with the startling impulsiveness which I soon learned was her characteristic, she hurled herself off me:

"*Ah, Vous n'etes pas Anglais*" she hissed. "*Vous ete espion. Sale cochon!*"

I was a dirty pig of a German spy.

Violence seemed about to follow when, in something quite near desperation, I remembered that in a wallet in my tunic I had a couple of photographs of myself pushed up in British uniform during my pre-prisoner era.

"*Attendez, s'il vous plait,*" croaked I. "*Je vous montre quelque chose.*"

And with some difficulty, for she had me flat on my back on the bed, I extricated the pictures. She eyed the photographs searchingly and when the effect had registered she literally cried penitence for her unjustified suspicions and accusations – and more vigorously than ever resumed her intentions in the way of romance. But further proceedings were abruptly interrupted by some loud raps on the door which signalled that Paul was becoming agitated by the lapse of time. Was I *fertig*, he asked, meaning was I ready to leave. Julie told Paul to go away in language I did not understand but which I am sure was very scurrilous. She clung to me until we were separated.

Although I suspect that Julie's work in the bar occasionally went beyond the serving of drinks I sincerely acknowledge, with gratitude, her good intentions towards me – or perhaps more exactly for the Flag I represented. Although I might have described our *rapprochement* with some levity, I shall always remember the genuine sentiment that motivated her reaction.

When I regained the truck with Paul I was greeted with some bawdy banter from my prisoner comrades who had been kept waiting in the vehicle outside the cafe. Peter, who had remained to keep watch on them, had meanwhile conveyed to them by descriptive gestures just what I was up to, or rather what he imagined I was.

"You're a lucky bastard," said a Canadian prisoner in the party.

"What the hell have you got that we haven't" added another, a Scotsman, with obvious envy.

I climbed into my usual place in the driving cab between

Peter and Paul, and affected a cheerful acceptance of their spicy sallies and enquiries concerning what had recently come my way. But in truth I was nauseated by the experience. It was all too sudden and brutal, and entirely devoid of the ideality required for alluring interludes. In the normal way I imagine I should have found the episode exciting and to some extent charming; but in the circumstances I have described, I'm afraid not.

One morning when I was nagging Imhof, the Commandant, about our multiple grievances he told me that we could shortly expect a woman interpreter for permanent duty at the depot. He added, with some heat, that I could then plague her with my perpetual moans. I did sense, however, that her appointment was not of his choosing and he hardly concealed his hostility to the idea. She duly turned up. A German born national, she was a woman in full middle age. For many years before the war, she told me, she had lived in London and had something to do with the catering business. I think she ran a Delicatessen.

"So you will understand that although I am really German, I have every sympathy with you boys who are prisoners," she assured me.

For the first few days she gave a ready ear to the prisoners' tales of their woes and even solicited them, but from the very beginning I had my suspicions.

She undoubtedly had been domiciled in London. That was pretty evident by her almost perfect command of English. Unfortunately for Germans who kept shops in England, however, some of them had a rough time from marauding mobs after unpeaceful incidents like Zeppelin raids, etc.

Most Germans, like the British, had their hearts in their country's interests, and she soon showed which side she was on. I felt quite certain that the woman was planted among us for "Intelligence" purposes, and one of my deep worries was that she would discover and expose the sabotage on the motor vehicles which the boys continued to inflict on an increasingly reckless scale. During our nightly clandestine "conferences" among the prisoners I often urged some caution but this was scornfully rejected by some of the more devil-may-care types of which there was no shortage in the Roubaix camp.

Before long my suspicions about the lady interpreter began to be appreciated by the men in the camp. After a while she was contemptuously referred to as The Old Frau, an appellation that was to become the usual reference when things were normal. But on the occasions when the boys thought she was up to her tricks she was known by epithets never applied to tender and virtuous ladies.

Something the Germans did discover, and took very serious notice of, was a series of mysterious depletions of their precious food rations supplied for the general Works, none of which were ever destined for the prisoners anyway. Some of us in the prison camp were well aware who caused these depredations. The culprits were in our midst. Some of the raids were epics in daring-do. For example, one night two of the prisoners somehow ascended and emerged through the lofty camp roof, then scaled the V roofs of three adjoining high buildings in order finally to wriggle through the glass roof of a fourth building where they helped themselves to as many bags of rice as they could struggle back with.

It required little imagination on my part to envisage The Old Frau spotting some of the rice grains on the floor and linking things up. In the event she missed the clues, but what she did notice, before she had been with us one week, was the Scots fellow Peebles with two semi-squashed tomatoes in his pocket. He had contrived to stray over to a patch of earth that was *verboten* where tomatoes and other vegetables were being coaxed to maturity. Peebles lifted what he could.

The Old Frau immediately reported him and very shortly afterwards two German guards took Peebles away for his punishment which was several days' solitary confinement on half his already starvation rations with cold water instead of "coffee" (which was burnt acorns anyhow).

The Old Frau had thus exposed her real mission with no delay, and this Peebles incident marked the beginning of a feud between us until we eventually separated. Her greater vantage point more than once landed me on the fringe of a sticky *finale*.

Naturally, but perhaps imprudently, I lost no time in confronting her about Peebles.

"I was only doing my duty by reporting him," she said.

"So this kind of snooping is your *duty*?" I asked her. "We were told you came as an interpreter."

"Do you know how severely Peebles has been punished as a result" I asked.

"Yes, I do," said she. "And he deserves it. He will not do it again."

"I suppose you will get the Women's Iron Cross for this" I sneered.

"Be careful, Tucker" she answered. "I warn you. I already know of some of your games." I had no doubt she did.

In direct ratio to the increasingly desperate food situation of the Germans we prisoners in unrecognized and unorganized camps suffered accordingly. Those in the established camps were receiving food parcels through the beneficent agency of the International Red Cross. But those of us whom the Germans had dumped just behind their fighting lines had been officially "believed killed" since early April. It was now the end of August and we could only trust that the camp address I had wrenched from the Germans would soon be brought to the official notice of those in England who had to do with the food parcels.

In the meantime sheer hunger was driving many of us to a barbaric state of living among ourselves. The behaviour of some prisoners when anything eatable showed up was below the level of a famished flock of birds hopping, squawking and pecking at one another when some bread crumbs are suddenly thrown in their midst. Potato peelings in garbage bins were rummaged out and not too carefully scraped, as well as any other refuse which could be made at all edible.

These conditions favoured The Old Frau with one more potential bar to her Iron Cross. One evening she detected Private Pat Mulligan of the Irish Fusiliers slightly beyond his prison bounds and in suspicious proximity to the hut that adjoined the German Food Kitchen. The Old Frau at once directed the German sentries to Mulligan's whereabouts. A search revealed nothing eatable in his pockets, but he had no right to be where he was and he was yanked before the Commandant for disciplinary treatment.

Under interrogation, however, it appeared that Mulligan invoked some kind of political immunity and, furthermore, he refused to accept The Old Frau's competence as the interpreter for the case. Would the Commandant kindly send for Tucker? So two German sentries, complete with fixed bayonets (the usual ritual when I had to cross the public road to the German Orderly Room) directed me to accompany them to the Commandant.

"I suppose you know why this man is before me," said Imhof.

"Yes I do," I replied. "But he was only taking a walk. He has done nothing wrong," I added.

"He was in a place that is *verboten* for prisoners," said Imhof. "But he says he is NOT AN ORDINARY PRISONER. What the hell is he talking about?"

I looked at Mulligan inquiringly.

"Tell him I'm NEUTRAL," said Pat. "I'm Irish, and nothing to do now with the British Army."

Considering that Pat was standing there in his British uniform, and had even managed to polish his cap badge which proudly identified him with the Irish Fusiliers, I thought his plea of diplomatic immunity was a rather stiff one for me seriously to put over on Imhof, a hard-boiled German warrior.

While I was puzzling out for a moment the best line I could take, The Old Frau interjected some comment on the facts.

"I don't want that bloody old cow in it," shouted Pat, an observation that rather understandably brought a scowl of annoyance on the lady's face.

I made signs to Mulligan to cool down and I must add that Imhof himself hinted to The Old Frau that her intervention was unnecessary.

I thereupon gestured to Imhof that Mulligan became temporarily deranged at times, through war experiences and the privations he was now unavoidably enduring. The officer and I exchanged knowing but surreptitious winks.

"So," said Imhof, throwing forward his arms in a manner which indicated he had heard enough and we could all clear out of his office. We did.

On the way back to the camp The Old Frau remarked that I had pulled a sly one and she added:

"He (Mulligan) is as sane as I am."

"That might be," I replied, "but it still leaves him a low mental rating."

My answer, I must confess, was very rude, but I was hopping mad with her.

"You insulting young swine," she howled. "I'll have you. You wait!"

"It is for *you* to wait," shouted Pat to her. He had just come within earshot. "I'll get something coming to you when this bloody lot is over," he added.

Which few words of perfect lucidity rather justified the lady's contention that Pat was not mentally disabled.

My once-weekly stint in the Works Office making up the pay sheets had become a slight relief from the dreary day-to-day existence. I was provided with a chair – an actual chair to sit on – a simple piece of furniture which it seemed ages since I had used. One of the office windows gave on to a public road where I saw evidence that the world of humanity was still in being, even if that world did have a surfeit of soldiers in grey-green.

Welcome, too, was the conversational opportunities with a few other men on indoor work, even if they also wore grey-green uniforms. In the main they were wounded soldiers who were now doing office work because they were unfit for further combat duties. And their wounds must have been serious before the German authorities would put them on recessive service, so acute was their man-power problem.

These men were almost all quite friendly with me, and sympathetic. One character with whom I had most contact was Charlot. I never knew his surname. He came from Alsace-Lorraine, the French territory that was acquired by Germany after the Franco-Prussian war of 1870. But the populace remained fiercely French by heart and its smouldering hostility to the Germans needed little fanning when the 1914 war broke out. (Herr von Jagow, the Police President of Berlin at the time, in a letter to the newspapers, described Alsace-Lorraine as "almost an enemy's country"). So when Charlot whispered to me –

"I am in the German Army; but I come from Alsace" he did not have to say any more.

Among Charlot's several duties for the German military administration he was an assistant to an Army doctor whose job it was to tour the French brothels for the purpose of the control and suppression of venereal disease. (I suppose that in Charlot I had met the living personification of that disesteemed and shadowy character referred to in barracks as a Pox Doctor's Clerk). Charlot gave me vivid descriptions of the *modus operandi* employed to examine the prostitutes, and I gathered that the examiners were not averse from using the amenities themselves once they were satisfied that the ladies were hygienically safe.

In common with most other Continental armies, the Germans dealt realistically with the venereal diseases problem. Prostitutes in the occupied countries were free to cater for the invaders – often encouraged to – provided they remained healthy, and the Germans provided sensible medical facilities to help them in this direction. But if the prostitutes accepted clients when there was any suspicion of infection the punishments were indeed severe.

The British, by contrast, showed a stupid attitude to life's realities in this context. In consequence they suffered a devastating casualty rate for their puritanism and hypocrisy. In the Middle East, for example, no less than one third of the troops there were incapacitated by venereal disease at one time, so I read in a book by one of the Allied officers on the services medical corps. Apart from the horrible physical incidence of a dose of gonorrhoea or syphilis, the men who got into trouble suffered cruel retribution by the authorities. In the early days, at any rate, their family allowances (in addition to their own pay) were stopped and their dependants (wives, or next of kin) were told why. Many an afflicted young soldier deliberately courted a sniper's bullet in preference to facing the inevitable ignomony.

It was said that the obstinate element in Britain responsible for the Puritan attitude was that *eminence gris* known as The Establishment, a largely civilian element sufficiently powerful to prevent the higher Army Command from introducing preventive prophylactic measures in the way the Germans and French did. Towards the end of the war, however, the ravages of venereal disease did force the British authorities to offer some remedial precautions. A prophylactic package was eventually issued to British troops (although I never saw one) in which a small phial of permangamate of potash predominated. Therewith was a short printed note to the effect that should the recipient be so tempted (bestial, not tempted, was the word really implied) to succumb to sexual intercourse, he should as soon as possible after that event seek the seclusion of a dark doorway or similar dim nook and douche his member from the phial of antiseptic potion.

With the Germans and French there were established properly equipped ablution posts at which their men could protect themselves with little more formality or thought than what attended any normal toilet operation.

It is certainly not to be inferred from what I have written that going with prostitutes was the regular thing with troops on active service. Indeed, the overwhelming majority of young fellows never sought or had the experience. For one thing, the necessary women were simply not available. For another, the men on active service were in places quite remote from such facilities. But the main deterrent was the idea of any physical contact with the female sexual automatons who did the service involved. But, understandably, there was that small minority of men who almost compulsively sought relief from sexual starvation. Those who took a sensible view of the problems agreed that something rational should be done about it.

Charlot was very helpful and friendly towards me as time went on. He would buy me occasional vegetables, tomatoes and other minor items from sources in Roubaix, for which I was able to pay him from the money I had secreted. To appreciate a tomato, however anaemic looking or decayed it might be, it is necessary to live for a few months with hunger perpetually gnawing at your vitals. Now and again Charlot also bought for me from a German soldier a packet of his army tobacco ration, or rather what passed as tobacco. It really was dried cherry-tree leaves which were then crisp and handled like wood shavings. I smoked this through the typical German pipe that was common in those days and had a bowl as big as a small teacup. I kidded myself that I was soothed by the process – until the result was near nausea.

XIV

HORS-D'ŒUVRE

It now transpired that Charlot was to introduce a subject which for me was momentous and, to some extent, lasting. Among the young ladies he knew in Roubaix – and I would guess that there were few he did not know – was an English girl. Her father was something in the textile line before the war and his business was overrun when the Germans invaded. The Germans put all civilians of either sex to work and this girl who Charlot knew, Teresa, chose teaching English to German officers in preference to menial work in the factories.

"I have told Teresa about you," said Charlot, "And she says she would like to know more about you."

Charlot then dealt at enthusiastic length on Teresa's attractions although he admitted, with evident wistfulness, that she rather kept him at arm's length. I sensed that Charlot thought that the opportunity of discussing an English soldier prisoner with Teresa, coupled with the fact that he himself was an Alsacien and not a German, would help soften the young lady towards him. So I stepped in.

"Would you take a little letter to Teresa from me?" I asked Charlot.

After meditating upon the grave risks of being implicated with a letter from an enemy prisoner to an enemy civilian and the alternative reward of the powerful introduction it gave him to Teresa, he agreed to do it. So there and then I hurriedly scribbled a few lines of greetings from me as a fellow national and some banal words of hope that some day we might meet. I handed the note to Charlot, who, furtively glancing around, folded my message into a tiny area and placed it in his pocket wallet.

The Germans were now winkling out every possible male for fighting line service. Although they were evidently short of skilled motor mechanics they had long ago removed all but the elderly fitters. Even among these, the slightest insubordination or defection could be the excuse for being transferred to the infantry in the trenches. It was a perpetual nightmare to the poor old mechanics.

In consequence of the yet undetected sabotage by the prisoners in the garages, a returned lorry which had piled up because of a loosened retainer bolt in the steering column under the chassis) caused a German fitter to be charged with negligence. His punishment was transfer to the trenches.

He was quite a decent fellow and I was really sad at what had befallen him, knowing the real culprits as I did, and that he was entirely blameless. We knew him as Heinrich, and I found a way of having a few words with him to say I was sorry he was leaving us.

In the course of our brief talk he said it was common knowledge that shoals of German prisoners were now falling into British hands. He wondered how they were being treated by our people. Taking a chance, I hinted that if I were in his place I would try to be taken prisoner by the English. I told him of our superiority in food and all conditions (which was perfectly true).

"If I am captured, may I tell them your name and regiment?" asked Heinrich.

"Certainly," I replied, "and what is more I will give you a note."

So at the first opportunity I pencilled this message : –

"Should Heinrich . . ., bearer of this note, be taken prisoner by the British, please treat him well because he was friendly and helpful to British prisoners of war held at Roubaix."

To this I added my full name and Army Unit. Heinrich was sent away a couple of days later, and I never heard of him again. On reflection I realized that I have taken some risk in giving him such a note but I thought little more of possible consequences at the time. Existing during an era when risks were an everyday part of life – or losing it – tended to dim one's perception of what in normal days would be appalling chances. But in fact I had let myself in for some anxious moments later on. Instead of keeping his mouth shut, as I felt sure he would if only for his own self respect, Heinrich confided the story to two or three of his close comrades.

Before long, one of them approached me for a similar note. I obliged. Then, one by one, the string of applicants grew until the business was alarming. Some of them were candid in that they had no intention of voluntarily giving themselves up to the

British: but in case they were captured ... well my note would surely ease their lot.

The full implications of the extent to which I had stuck my neck out began to dawn on me. If I refused to issue the notes *ad lib*, any of the applicants could denounce me for what was common knowledge I had done. If any of them were killed or wounded in their own lines my note would have been discovered by the Germans, and in that event I knew that the Wall would be my sentence. Moreover, The Old Frau had only to stumble on the news, and that would have been my lot.

Early one bright morning a German guard came to escort me to the Commander Imhof. This worthy chief in fact required my presence nearly every day, sometimes several times a day, to iron out grievances by both sides but almost entirely by the prisoners. This morning's grievance, however, turned out to be a German one. As I marched along with my escort I made out, in the distance, the figures of Imhof and The Old Frau, both eyeing and pointing at a wall. This particular wall served as the prisoners' urinal and it was a simple concrete erection about 7 ft high by 10 ft wide. It faithfully obeyed the Continental contention that this particular excrementary function demanded no privacy where males were concerned.

As I got nearer the wall I gathered that a large portrait in chalk was claiming the attentions of Imhof and The Old Frau and they were trying to read aloud the inscription thoughtfully provided.

In close proximity, I saw this:—

WILHELM
FUCK HIM

Although anonymity completely cloaked the artist's identity, the effort shrieked its origin as the *chef d'œuvre* of a prisoner, and a British prisoner to boot.

"Tucker, what does that mean," roared Imhof at me as soon as I was within earshot of him.

It required no effort at all on the part of this German officer to look formidable. That was his natural appearance; but now, in addition, he was making most menacing gestures. I began to fear that I personally was in for a bashing. Imhof really was beside himself and was darting agitated glances at all quarters as if he expected the Kaiser himself, the hero of this portrait, suddenly to turn up.

I shrugged my shoulders once or twice – a dodge of mine to gain a little time.

"FUCK HIM *Was soll dies alles heissen?*" yelled the Commandant, demanding of me what it all meant.

How could I correctly translate it? I doubt if the expression is even capable of literal translation into English. Those of us at all familiar with things plebeian are perfectly aware of its insulting meaning without having the slightest idea of its definition.

Anyway, I rather falteringly told Imhof that the words could mean a term of endearment. I admit, however, that only a very naïve student of biology would have supported my "explanation".

The Commandant was unconvinced. He remained ferocious and scandalized by our artist's conception of His Imperial Highness on the urinal wall and was so far unmoved by my efforts to tone down the affront.

He threatened to inflict punishment on the entire prison unless he was given the name of the culprit. I knew very well he would never get it. I also knew that the threatened punishment would take the form of a reduction in our already scanty rations.

As time went on quite a few of the prisoners had wandered along to use the urinal. By accurately aiming their releases direct at the noble Wilhelm II they by no means aided my endeavours to conciliate the Commandant. The Old Frau was no soothing influence either. She kept up a continual nagging, in German to Imhof and in English to me, that the whole affair was the most disgusting insult to her Emperor that she could have ever imagined.

After an uncomfortable time at the receiving end of Imhof's anger and threats he eventually cooled down a bit and accepted my undertaking that the prisoners themselves would immediately wash away the offending effort and would deal with the culprit who had caused such trouble. If they didn't, Imhof warned, and/or if anything of the kind happened again there would be the direst consequences.

In due course I let my fellow prisoners know in no uncertain terms that it was no joke being answerable to the Commandant for this kind of prank. I hope that our artist, whoever he was, would in future express his sense of humour in directions that would not incite so much German wrath. I am afraid, however, that the whole camp would have been delighted to see the episode repeated *ad infinitum*.

XV

TERESA

"I have a little letter for you from Teresa," said Charlot to me on entering the office to do the paylists one morning.

I excitedly read a cheerful little note mainly composed of sweet nothings from an English girl in German occupied territory to an English boy prisoner of war. It bore no address and was initialled simply "T". But it delighted me immensely. It seemed such a magic and romantic talisman in the circumstances; indeed a link with any cultured humanity that remained and the beastly existence I was daily enduring. Charlot then followed with a few words that really took my breath away. He explained that I had been the subject of much conversation between Teresa and him and she had finally persuaded him to have a go at getting me to a place where she could pick me up, after which she would take care of the future.

"If you can get outside the camp into the main street outside, I will be there waiting for you and I will take you to Teresa," promised Charlot. He named the spot where he would be and the time would be 6.30 p.m. the following evening.

The assumption that I would get outside the camp – just like that – could, in the normal way, be considered as about as feasible as thrusting oneself into space orbit without rocket aid from the ground, and I am sure now that Charlot doubted that I would even attempt it. He was wrong.

A fairly big civilian labour force had been impressed for work at the garages adjoining the prisoners camp, and there were day and night shifts. The day shifts left the garage at about 6 p.m. It was hopeless of course for me to get through the outside gates without disguise. Because I was escorted daily outside the camp by guards on the way to the Commandant's office, all the gate sentries knew me quite well. With this in mind my one chance was to mix myself up with the French civilian workers, most of whom seemed to live in blue overalls (the French don't mind what colour it is as long as it *is blue*) and a cloth cap. The caps of those days, especially the French ones, were of terrific circumference. The material they used would be sufficient for a cap and an overcoat as well these days. Blue overalls I had already acquired, and I lost no time in scrounging one of these caps from one of the French workers I knew. That particular cap was even more voluminous than usual and when one side of it was pulled down *a la mode* I looked more like a music hall *apaché* than an Anglo-Saxon prisoner of war.

My being the go-between and hack-of-all-jobs for the prisoners and the Germans allowed me a little latitude around the camp precincts, and at about 6 p.m. on this notable evening I furtively loitered near the foreign workers. I mingled among them as they shuffled towards the exit gates, slowly past an entrance keeper in his box who, to my intense relief, scrutinized no passes and ... I was outside – FREE. But Freedom has several shades of qualification, as I was to learn. I unobtrusively but lightheartedly made my way to the spot appointed by Charlot for our rendezvous and waited very impatiently for 6.30 p.m. to come. It came. So did 7.30 p.m; and 8.30 p.m. But no Charlot. The street in which I was waiting became increasingly thronged with German soldiers either going places or occupying tables put out on the paveway by the cafés in traditional French custom. With a *Pardon, messieur* a café waitress actually moved me in order to place a table on the spot where I was waiting, there to accommodate four German troopers.

Charlot had let me down. But what was I to do now? I was now "free", but if I moved far I would almost certainly be picked up. Roubaix at that time was heavily garrisoned. German military police were very active, especially at key points, and questioned any civilian. More seriously, the first prerequisite of any escape plan was some reserve of food. Charlot had led me to believe that this exigency would be looked after. In any case we had so far had such limited rations that any saving of them was out of the question.

Hunger was in fact troubling me at that very time. It was approaching 9 p.m., when I should have to decide what to do. At that hour one of the night shifts of the French and foreign civilian workers *entered* the depot. So when they began to arrive and assemble outside I repeated the same furtive mingling with them, shuffled past the armed sentries and then past the entrance keeper in his box. This time the workers showed cards. With me, of course, that was a serious deficiency; but in the gloom I squirmed through and ... into the camp. The entrance keeper yelled something at me about the pass-card, which I later learned was shown and stamped for the purpose of time-keeping if the holder would receive his pay. So I lost my pay for the "shift".

I ruefully resumed my prison routine. When I next saw Charlot I was of course very uncordial. He countered my scorn and reproach with the simple confession:

"Sorry, Tommy. At the last moment my nerve went."

Towards the end of August I was the happy recipient of a terse piece of information from the German Commandant that would transform our lot. It meant more to us than anything we had heard since becoming prisoners more than four months previously. It was that food parcels had arrived. They were then at the Belgian town of Tournai and would be redirected to us as soon as transport could be made available.

These parcels were the result of the generous and noble efforts of several Welfare organizations in Britain. Mine was donated by the National Cyclists Union. Their conveyance to the prisoners was arranged by the International Red Cross, to which any prisoner will raise his hat to the end of his days.

The contents of these parcels were intelligently planned. They included many edible and nourishing commodities that could be preserved in tins or packets, as well as tobacco and cigarettes. It is not stretching the truth to record that these parcels saved many a prisoner from starvation, because by September 1918 the Germans themselves were desperately suffering through lack of nourishment. What, therefore, was left for prisoners requires no imagination.

These parcels also made many an escape possible. An exacting indispensable of any escape plan was some reserve of portable food and this was impossible to save from the meagre prison rations given to us by the Germans, even supposing that the kind of food issued would remain edible, which it would not. From the parcels, however, a small store of biscuits and chocolate could be reserved (with painful effort) for the get-away chance that always hovered in our imaginations.

When the first parcels did arrive – about one week after we were told about them – there were only 24, and the effect of the disappointment on the 230 or so who didn't get them was indeed shocking. The parcels were each addressed by name to individual prisoners. Those who received them never dreamed of sharing the contents – even supposing that 24 parcels could have been amicably shared among 260 mouths. The result was an ugly scuffle; the kind of hideous fracas that can only too easily and suddenly boil up among a batch of famished, cooped up and deprived males.

Most of the prisoners at once got the idea that their parcels had been stolen upon arrival in German hands, for it was realized only too readily what a temptation they must have presented to whoever might handle them. So my comrades charged me with the onerous job of conveying their suspicions to the Commandant and to persuade him to arrange some way of ensuring the safe transmission of the precious food parcels. In other words, I was to tell Imhof that our parcels were being pilfered by his compatriots. I was spared having to put over that sour message because news of the riot in the camp over the parcels had preceded me. To my relief the Commandant was understanding and sympathetic, and he undertook to let me go to the arrival depot in Tournai personally to check the parcels as soon as he received notification of the next batch.

I never did find any evidence whatever that a single parcel had in fact been lifted by the Germans. On the contrary, the only instances of theft that came to my notice were committed by the prisoners themselves. *All* the men subsequently received personal parcels from succeeding arrivals. The Commandant honoured his promise and in due course the ubiquitous two German soldiers, fully armed, escorted me to the Goods Receiving Depot via a street car from Roubaix to Tournai. The presence of a British prisoner caused much excitement among the civilian tram passengers and although my German guards would not allow any fraternization they appeared to enjoy that they were part of the commotion.

On leaving the tram to wherever I was being taken, I was piloted in file by my escorts, one in front of me and one at the back, across the spacious cobbled place *en face* the impressive Tournai Cathedral. My presence was very much noted by the civilian crowds milling around this rendezvous; but I'm afraid I presented no dashing and joyous example of a *soldat Anglais.* Much as I was revelling in my temporary release among this outside world of active humanity I was being led along on a leash as it were, and suffering the sense of humiliation that is felt by all military prisoners.

But, crossing this Cathedral place, I was suddenly, if momentarily, highly exhilarated. A man passing the opposite way deliberately brushed against me and said:

"Cheer up Mate! Won't be long now." His accent was unmistakably Cockney. Despite my surprise I looked fixedly ahead. Both my guards turned immediately around, but the fellow had evidently managed to bury himself in the crowd. I wondered who he might be and what he was up to. During the next few weeks I was to meet a few characters of the same stamp as I imagined him to be, whose underground exploits in the guerilla world made fictional heroics no more thrilling than a Sunday School tea party.

When one morning a German non-commissioned officer as well as a sentry picked me up at the camp to escort me to the office of the Polizei I feared the worst. The mere word Polizei struck an understandable chill among those in occupied territory. Was I about to be confronted with one of those notes I was giving to Germans who might fall in Allied hands? That, I thought, was my only misdemeanour serious enough to interest the German police.

It was by now common knowledge among the German army mechanics in the motor depot that if they were transferred to the trenches it was as well to get a "pass" from me. So I could not be surprised if at any time someone or something let the cat out of the bag — in which event I had no illusions about the consequences.

I now really had the jitters every time the Commandant sent for me. And now that the Polizei had named me . . . well I hardly breathed again until I found the subject to be more agreeable.

On the way to the office I managed to worm out from my escorts a vague idea of the object of my summons. The ordinary guards were usually about as communicative as turnips, probably from fear. But the N.C.O., who happened to know me slightly through my working in the pay office (and who probably knew Charlot) gave me the surprising tip-off that my "fiancée" was with the German police in the Commandant's office.

Although I was very mystified by the 'fiancée' aspect — I was nowhere near being betrothed to anyone — I guessed right away that something was going on with Teresa as the life of the party and she was using the fiancée tag in order to wangle the meeting.

On arrival at the office I faced our Commandant and one of the Polizei. Imhof simply but sternly said to me:

"Tucker! Your fiancée has asked permission to see you."

"I should be very grateful for your permission," I replied.

I did my best to react in a matter-of-fact and convincing way but I thought it too much to believe that Imhof was taken in by the charade and did not even query the circumstances in which I could become affianced to Teresa: or the astonishing coincidence which found two people, already engaged to be married, to be both prisoners of war in the same town. Surely Imhof and the Polizei were not so naïve as to swallow this one. They must be deliberately letting the game go on because they thought they might uncover something in the wind that was anti-German?

"I give you two minutes with her," said Imhof, and with a *"Kom mit"* he opened the door to an adjoining office. And there was Teresa! I shall never forget my impressions – a vivid highlight among my memories. When the Commandant opened the door she was facing the opposite way and was not aware of us for a few seconds. Involved in some altercation with two German military police, she seemed in complete command of the situation and was emphasizing some aspects of her contentions with vigorous jabs of a small, decorative walking stick she carried.

When she wheeled around and saw me she almost gasped the exclamation "Willy!" (her version of William, my first name) and immediately made towards me, arms outstretched. Since I took it to be customary for fiancés to kiss when they meet again after a long separation, whatever the circumstances, and no matter who might be looking, we enacted a passionate embrace. I am no actor; I was trembling. But I hope I carried my part manfully, if not a la Don Juan. As for Teresa; well, no actress has done better.

The Commandant had previously warned Teresa that we had only two minutes for our tryst and so she hurriedly asked me for my home address in case she was repatriated first. I gave her the address of my elder brother in London as the person who could most suitably react.

I was now becoming more fully aware of one of the most attractive and vivacious young ladies it had been my fortune to know, when Imhof abruptly ruptured my rapturous ecstasy with his order: "Tucker: *Gehe hinter,*" which, in the way he said it, meant that I was to get the hell out of it, and quickly too. There was no misunderstanding the order on the part of my escorts, either. They hustled me, none too gently, away from my charmer and straight back to the unromantic confines of the prison precincts.

This girl certainly showed the Germans what used to go for British precocity. She must have given her parents some terrifying hours. I learnt later on from a letter she sent me when the war was over, that after my abortive attempt to reach her the night Charlot let us down, she decided to beard the German Commandant and ask his permission to see me. In the first place she asked if she could send me a little packet of tobacco, with a short note inside.

"My word! You should have seen his eyes. I did not ask twice." I quote from Teresa's letter, which I still have.

"Have you not seen the recent notice?" demanded the officer. He referred to an unfriendly edict which threatened death among other dire incidentals for having any contact with the enemy.

"Of course I have," replied Teresa, "I don't walk about with my eyes shut."

"But," she pleaded, "let me see just one of them."

"Which one?" asked the officer.

"Willy Tucker," replied Teresa.

Since it happened that the Commandant (Imhof) knew this particular prisoner fairly well, the going began to be very dicey. What contact had there been between the two of them while they were in German hands? At this point Teresa took her chance.

"He is my fiancé," she lied. And her begging and coaxing evidently wore down the rugged Commandant to the extent that he capitulated and had me brought over. But he took the precaution of advising the German Polizei, which explains the presence of the police in this little to-do.

What prompted Teresa to do all this? As she had never seen or spoken to me there could have been no element of affection to induce the fiancé myth. So I can only infer that it was a desperate urge to gain some contact of any kind with a fellow national who was also deprived of normal liberty.

In spite of the many instances of hard going between Imhof and I over prison camp troubles, I like to think that he gave way on this occasion with Teresa, and took some risk in so doing, because of a little friendly tolerance. For my part I harboured no rancour against him.

In 1919, both Teresa and I found ourselves in England by separate and devious ways. We had much to do with each other from then onwards, and I still have letters from her in New Zealand where she lives, over 50 years after we met in Roubaix.

Any normal male will readily appreciate the unsettling and mercurial repercussions this encounter with Teresa had for me. Here was I, a young man deprived of his liberty in conditions of depravity that no civil prisoners had to endure whatever their crimes, and excluded on pain of extinction from humanity at large; when out of the blue I am kissing a fascinating and beautiful young woman who calls me her sweetheart! Marvellous as was the episode, it plunged me into a bottomless depression from which I could see no respite, even by escaping. If I got out again I did not know where Teresa lived, and even if I did I most certainly could not expose her to the death penalty by approaching her and giving her the responsibility of hiding me or getting me clear.

For the better part of the next two days I could think of nothing else but ways and means of shaking off my intolerable fetters and becoming free; all the plans of course being framed with fugitive meetings with Teresa in mind. Finally I decided to throw myself on what suggestions Charlot might have in this direction. I would promise him as much monetary bribery as I could rake up, if he really would lend me his personal help. Alas, my meetings with Charlot (in the pay office) were limited to once a week, and there were then three more long, interminable days to go before the next time.

But changes occur even in the humdrum, seemingly static existence of prisoners of war. Every day the rumble of front line war crept nearer to Roubaix. Nearly every night now our British planes were swooping to roof top height. We prisoners lived in blissful imagination that our airmen knew exactly where we were and we welcomed their near-miss bombs in fancied safety, perfect comfort, and even delight. We learned different. When raids were in progress the prisoners would contrive to disturb black-out arrangements and even open doors, the idea being to show what light they could. I think they all realized there was no sense in doing that, but the urge to be awkward was paramount. Our German guards, scared and furious, would push us around, yelling something like "*Lös, lös, die flieger komt*".

On a morning following some ominous evidence of the inexorable British advance the Commandant instructed me to tell the prisoners that they would be quitting Roubaix that very same day for another destination. That news meant little more to them beyond gathering together their humble possessions into a sack or wrapping in readiness for the move. There could hardly be less ceremony about a prisoner's removal.

So not long afterwards, we were herded and then crammed into a small convoy of motor lorries and driven off. In the ordinary way we should have had to trudge the journey, no matter how long. Transport was used simply because the Germans were in haste to get it beyond reach of the Allies (in case of a break through) and it made sense to load the trucks with prisoners.

For my comrades the move meant nothing. It was merely a matter of another miserable location for captivity. But for me it meant the end of Teresa, and I never remember being more downhearted. In the truck in which I travelled I was thrust in the driving cabin aside the German driver. For miles all I could imagine dancing on the glass windscreen was the pretty, smiling face of Teresa. Yet could I have foreseen the turn of events at the next destination, that journey along the monotonous, tree lined, wartime roads of Northern Flanders would certainly not have assumed the forlorn wrench that it did.

XVI

ENGHIEN and MADELEINE

That journey ended at Enghien, formerly a pleasant town in Belgium, about 18 miles south-west of Brussels. A school building of fair size had been hurriedly bodged up as a prison, a conversion which meant merely that it was denuded of all furniture or any amenity, artificial or natural, that goes for part of normal living. On the other hand there was added a plenitude of locks and bars and spikes and barbed wire.

On arrival at the building we prisoners just flopped on the floor more or less where we happened to stop. Except for a preference to settle against a wall, where possible, there was little point in being choosey. But once having dumped yourself down, that particular two or three square yards was inviolate. No other prisoner would normally poach the position.

Our guards here were elderly *Landstürmers* again, too old or unfit for the rigours of combat. They were reasonable fellows, generally speaking, except that they handled their rifles in a rather too zealous and constant state of fancied emergency. On both sides you could almost always pick out at once the actual war-scarred chaps by the way they carried their rifles. Those who had been through it slung their rifle carelessly over their shoulders with about as much thought for it as if it had been a pencil. But those who had not been mixed up in the real stuff always had their fire-arms poised as though they had already taken aim and it was now just a matter of pulling the trigger.

The Germans, having shifted our camp in a hurry, either gave no thought at all to the problem of continuing even their parsimonious issue of rations, or they had become hopelessly disorganized. Imhof, the Rubaix Commandant, had not followed to Enghien with us. Some of the Top Brass among the German officers in Enghien asserted authority over us but I could get absolutely no news or satisfaction from them about bread or the crudest necessities.

There was no garage work here, but the prisoners were made to form parties to man-handle heavy consignments that were to be loaded or unloaded at Enghien railway station. In desperation at the food rations position, the prisoners decided to have another go at "strike" action. One afternoon, after being formed up in what was once the school playground, they stood their ground and refused to move off for work at the railway station when the German order came to do so. When they realized what was afoot, the old trigger-happy *Landstürmers* pranced around in something like Gilbert & Sullivan panic. Yelling the eternal "*Lös, Lös*" they began persuading our men to get going with their rifle butts. Before long there was one confused mêlée of German guards and prisoners, with the caps and headgear of both sides being trampled underfoot.

Although there had been much shoving and cursing, no one had been really hurt. But the German wrath was mounting. One of the guards grasped the muzzle of his rifle and, swinging it above his head, made as if to crash it on the person of Gunner Barlow, a hefty ex-member of the Royal Artillery. Eyeing the rifle aloft, Barlow measured a punch with his big, clenched fist. Snarling "Gertchyer, you Jerry bastard," he lunged at the belligerent *Landstürmer*, but missed. Absolutely astounded, the guard lost hold on his rifle, which crashed to the ground at both their feet. Whereupon it was Barlow who picked it up and, with a courteous gesture, gently handed it back to the German.

After a lot of noise, the prisoners sullenly shambled off to their labours, but their practical protest was not without effect. The Old Frau, who had seen the affray, lost no time in bringing the news to the notice of the German officer adminstering Enghien. Her purpose no doubt was to invoke some punishment for the incident, but it did not work out like that. The German high rankers were becoming increasingly mindful that they might not, after all, win this war. The Enghien Commander gave a hearing to my strong protest on the conditions of the prisoners and even took my hint that the Allied Command might be in a position before long to question those responsible for subjecting their prisoners of war to privations which were so gravely contrary to international law.

The prisoners were *not* punished for their mutinous action. Further, the officer promised he would cause us to receive a regular ration of bread which I personally could see collected daily – a proviso that had now become a very necessary precaution since even this awful black compound they called *brot* was rationed in half-ounces, so desperate was the food shortage.

The good civilians of Enghien quickly and energetically

reacted to the fact that they now had, for the first time, some 250 British prisoners of war captive in their town. They, being more informed than we, were increasingly alive to the apparent coming turn in the fortunes of war. This encouraged and emboldened them to become daring in their efforts to help British prisoners in every way they could. It was still a grave risk for them to do so, however, and the Germans remained pretty ruthless with their deterrents. But through their indefatigable Mayoress, a middle-age lady still with youthful charm and beauty despite her wartime cares and six children, the Enghien people made known to us (via got-at German guards) their wish to help us and provide us with what amenities they could. This excepted basic foods, of course, since they themselves could procure only the barest essentials.

Bombardier Leaver, who was once something in the entertainment line, and who had much to do with our camp theatricals at Roubaix, asked if they could let us have a piano and a very good piano was spirited into the prison the day following the request. For good measure, the worthy Mayoress also sent in several theatrical make-ups which included one girl's wig of luxuriant golden hair. Thereupon our comrade Leaver and his entertainment committee lost no time in arranging musical concert parties among the prisoners. These mainly took the form of sketches, shanties, transcriptions and parodies of popular ditties, most of which took the Mickey out of our Teutonic captors in a most uninhibited and scurrilous manner.

The camp entertainment committee decided that I should wear the wig and be made up as a girl for the concert parties. They did not say what they used for cosmetics or how they came by some of the "négligé", but after they had done with me there emerged a comely wench. Her voluptuous curves drew whistles of admiration even though her most prominent contours were old rags. This sexual metamorphosis was in fact too devastating for some of my frustrated comrades. I was compelled to take evading action and ward off several loving embraces. Indeed things became so no-joke that I finally insisted on having a man's part if they wanted me in future shows, and as I was the only one in the camp who could do anything with the piano my wishes had to be accepted.

The school playground was almost ringed by local houses but the high surrounding wall (it might have been a prison before it was a school) just prevented the residents from seeing what went on behind. The prisoners thought it would be an excellent idea to make it possible for the tenants of the houses to see our first concert show, seeing that those people had made the thing possible.

"No problem at all," said a couple of our fellows who were once in the building trade. And, using some school benches and junk rummaged from goodness knows where, they arranged a stage sufficiently spacious for the six performers and the piano. This they elevated six feet above ground level, the height necessary to give the locals a grand-stand view. "Exits","Entrances" and "Dressing" were underneath the stage, out of sight of the houses. Moreover, the stage was portable or, more precisely, capable of being quickly erected or dismantled. It was deemed advisable not to inform the Germans about the Show before it was actually in progress.

By this time I had become wise to the devious ways and means of underground communication in Enghien under the noses of our captors and I was able to send news to the Mayoress of our forthcoming show and that we hoped to entertain the residents of the houses surrounding the school yard. Curtain Up: 7 p.m. the following evening.

And at that hour every window and vantage point swarmed with the local inhabitants, who waved and generally gesticulated their enthusiasm. Up went the stage, then the piano, followed by me on the piano stool. I promptly hammered out my idea of a musical overture comprising the pop ditties of that time, which lent themselves much more to communal singalongs than today's rages. Our audience at the windows joined in with gusto, and the German occupation troops in the town just could not credit their ears as hundreds of local voices joyfully and noisily joined in well-known choruses for the first time since the jackboot invasion.

Then came a musical sketch which, alas, did not reach its intended finale. It was the middle of a specially transcribed song, soulfully rendered by baritone Fusilier Eaton and murdered on the piano by me. The theme was the music and basis of *A little bit of Ireland fell out the Sky one Day.* The singer was just lamenting that A little bit of *Sauerkraut* fell out the Sky one Day, when the lid of the piano was suddenly slammed down – and I was lucky to clear my hands in time. Shouting "*Lös, lös, es verboten ist*", one of the German guards had vaulted aloft and interrupted the performance.

The civilian audience hissed and booed its displeasure and the prisoner audience sung its defiance to the air of another well known hymn:

"When this bloody war is over
Oh how happy I shall be
When I get back to dear old Blighty
No more *Sauerkraut* for me
I will tell the German major
To stick his black bread . . ."

The guards reached the singing prisoners just as the destination of the black bread was about to be suggested . . . and the performance was suspended. But we prisoners had our first good laugh for a long time from it. And so, we learned, did the Belgians.

Precisely when the building in which we were held ceased being used as a school I do not know, but the Belgian superintendent and his wife continued to live in the school house about 100 yards distant. The same land area accommodated both buildings, but now that the school was a prison the house was isolated by wire barricades and other obstacles.

The superintendent had a daughter and the news that she was unusually attractive had well and truly percolated the supposedly impenetrable confines of the prison camp in a way that amply confirmed the classic tag that anything to do with love laughs at locksmiths. The boys even knew her name: Madeleine. I personally was late in becoming aware of her. I was still representing the boys, like I had at Roubaix, and the carnival of tasks that befell me kept me perpetually occupied.

The Old Frau was still much in evidence and she kept a constant eye on our misdemeanours, especially those she considered to be mine.

Twice daily, 8.00 in the morning and 8.30 at night, she would physically count the prisoners to make sure none was missing. Her routine was to contact me, in order that I would arrange the chaps in some kind of formation that facilitated a count. Or so she hoped. But these were never any exhibitions of military precision and she always ended up by guessing rather than counting. These were also the occasions for me to deluge her with a shoal of moans about our lot – and for her to retaliate with threats of grim consequences as a result of the many deviations by the prisoners from the straight and narrow paths permitted to *kriegsgefangeners*.

The German officer commanding Enghien had assured me that in addition to arranging the renewal of our bread ration he would allow me personally to check that the allotted number of loaves did indeed arrive without some being missing. He kept his promise. The correct number of loaves was delivered daily by the Germans to the cellar of a house on the opposite side of the road (appropriately named the Rue d'Ecole) from the school. Every morning one of the German sentries, complete with the usual rifle, would escort me through the school gates to the bread cellar. There I could make my count and then arrange for delivery to my corner in the prison where our committee would cut and apportion the loaves to the queuing prisoners with an exactitude which could not be surpassed in a Mint dealing with gold ingots.

On the morning following our disrupted Concert Show, the German guard called for me to enact this bread ceremony in the usual way. A passage led from the front street door to the stairs of the cellar and on the right of that passage lay the kind of room known as the parlour in our own small Victorian houses.

The guard happened to be ahead of me and was descending the cellar when I noticed a winsome young lady in the parlour making covert signs to me. I dodged quickly aside to her and she at once somewhat furtively handed me a little packet which I hurriedly stowed into my pocket without saying a word. I then followed the guard into the cellar for the bread counting ritual.

Back in my corner of the prison I pulled out the little packet, expecting to find a tiny eatable of some kind – perhaps a morsel of home made pastry such as the local people would prepare themselves and try to give to prisoners. Instead, there was just a scribbled pencilled note in English, reading:

"Tommy. Get out of the window marked X at 20.00 hours tonight. Then wait.   M".

M. was the renowned Madeleine. Underneath this writing was a rough sketch showing this window marked X. Wrapped in this note was a white-metal finger ring, such as might be in a Christmas bon bon. Its purpose on this occasion was apparently more romantic than practical.

Now this part of Belgium was notorious for underground anti-German activities. Daily executions by the occupying invaders served only to intensify the acts of sabotage by the civilian Belgians, who regarded their erstwhile conquerors with a degree of loathing and hatred probably exceeding that shown by any of the other occupied countries, intense though they all were.

In the last year of the war, escape plans for Allied prisoners reached a particularly high state of efficiency. Every conceivable exigency, even synchronized stop-watches, were employed to avoid possible failure – as well they might, since it was almost invariably a simple alternative of success or death for those involved.

It was therefore an unwritten code of honour that any prisoner who "got the message" must go through with the attempt whatever the consequences or the risks or even if failure was starkly obvious from the beginning.

So when the call chose me I had no alternative, and neither did I seek one. In fact I felt flattered and rather invigorated by the opportunity.

I made a bee line for the appointed "X" window to survey the problems of getting out of it. It was immediately above the particular patch chosen by one Rifleman Hollowbone whereon to sleep (once a chap had pegged out his chosen "ground" on a prison floor, that rectangle of about 5 sq. ft was his indisputable dungheap for the duration of his stay in the prison). In those circumstances I was compelled to divulge to Holly (our nickname for Hollowbone) just why I was very interested in that window. Holly, by a stroke of wonderful luck for my immediate purpose, was a carpenter in North London before he joined the Army. To my relief and surprise he assured me he would find it no problem to force open the window without noise or removal of glass (I began to wonder whether burglary rather than woodwork was his pre-war vocation), and he swore his full cooperation and secrecy.

One serious complication was that at 20.30 hours it was the nightly and solemn routine of The Old Frau to enter the camp and seek my company in order to count the camp. However, Holly said he could force the window in advance in a way that it would stay quite unnoticed until the appointed time of my exit.

It was now gradually dawning on me that however noble were my Belgian accomplices outside, they were virgin novices in the technique of organizing escapes. A full moon and an armed sentry on constant patrol formed a sinister combination which of course no experienced escape group would ever dream of incurring. For all that, my participation was inexorably fixed. Whatever happened, the "message" had to be obeyed. That was the unwritten but relentless law of the prison camp and anyone who ratted on it would lead an intolerable existence thereafter.

As I watched a whale of a moon rise I bemused that any G. H. Elliot songs about Silvery Moons would in future be pure anathema to me; and when at about 7.30 p.m. its sheer brilliance outdid daylight in the clearest and most cloudless sky I have ever beheld, I wondered how anyone could possibly associate such ghastly phenonema with anything romantic.

Two or three minutes before the crucial moment, Holly noiselessly raised the window so that I could spot the sentry. The window was near the right hand corner of the building. The sentry was then at the extreme left of the building and was just wheeling round to retrace his steps. He was armed, of course, with rifle slung. He also carried a powerful torch, which the full moon had so far rendered unnecessary. He showed no signs of undue vigilance and sauntered almost nonchalantly along his beat. Breathlessly I waited for him to pass beneath my window and make his return. As soon as this did happen, and his back was towards me, I wriggled out and dangled with my hands clutching the window ledge. In due course the sentry had arrived at the extreme left of his beat again and had turned. By this time, also, The Old Frau had entered the camp, and was seeking me, half an hour earlier than her usual routine time. She even wandered over to the actual window under which I was hanging from its ledge.

"Where is Tucker" she asked Holly.

"He was here just now," he truthfully replied, "but he went outside down there," he untruthfully added. *Down there* was the camp latrine. The Old Frau thereupon hied herself off in the direction indicated, but as the lavatory in question was an outstanding example of the look-and-be-damned freedom then considered normal in that line, even The Old Frau could not stick such candour for long and she moved outside.

It has since occurred to me that those little angels who traditionally hovered above crazy war prisoners such as me must have put in some extra flying hours that night, because The Old Frau, although very annoyed at not finding me, cleared off for the rest of the night, a wholly exceptional happening. Had she remained and found me really missing she would vigorously and gleefully have let loose the entire formidable German paraphernalia for the recapture of wayward prisoners. All this I learned later, of course.

Meanwhile the sentry had retraced his steps once more, turned, and was on his way back along his beat again. Now was the moment for me to let go, and drop. I did. The window ledge was not really very high off the ground and I had only about 4ft. to fall. Had I known it – as I was destined to later that night – there was a way down from the window by way of ledges and protuberances in the brickwork.

However, I let go, and dropped. My left leg stuck in one side of a low stubbly bush. This caused me to lose my balance and fall somewhat heavily on my left shoulder. The sentry was now ambling nearby again. I could see him in the moonlight and I lay motionless until he strode away again.

"You-must-walk-like-a-very-old-man-now," whispered a girl's voice, in slow, stacatto words. My startled senses made me aware of Madeleine, who had secreted herself in nearby shrubs awaiting my arrival. She deftly threw a dark blanket around my shoulders. She had brought this along with the idea of cloaking any brass buttons on my army tunic. Obeying a sign to follow her, I silently walked bent-backed along a narrow track that led to the house of the school superintendent (her father) where she lived.

Madeleine's mother evidently knew what was afoot. Father didn't, and when he clapped eyes on me with Madeleine I have a vivid recollection of seeing a man shocked to the extreme and in great fear. I must allow that he certainly had every reason to be greatly alarmed, since the penalty inflicted by the Germans on those implicated in such goings on seldom allowed any earthly possibility of further misdemeanour. It was the firing squad. For all that, the imperturbable Madeleine sat me down at a table and found me a cup of hot soup, followed by a small chunk of unsweetened cake. No banquet at Claridges could have attracted me more. She spoke fluent English, with that devastating accent that has undone so many Englishmen. She fascinated me so much that I lost all awareness of the purpose for which I was on this mission. I could only gather, in a dreamy kind of way, that I, a creature who half an hour ago was out of circulation in human estimation, was now the object of this beautiful young lady's intentions.

I was vaguely aware that Madeleine calmly proceeded to explain her plans to the others for my get-away and she made the operation sound hardly more consequential than if she proposed to go to a shop up the road to buy some cabbages. I had to rig myself up as a girl, she said. She got that idea through seeing me at that concert show in my golden wig. She had already procured something like a wig. The clothing was no problem, she added. She would personally conduct me thus garbed to a rendezvous near the Dutch frontier, about 50 miles distant, where she could hand me over to a regular Escape Organization who would arrange my final deliverance.

Madeleine's poor father listened, aghast and temporarily inert. As for me, I gradually became aware of an all-pervading stimulation that would have sent me braving with delight any hazard connected with this glamorous young lady ... until my senses awoke to the suggestion that I submerge that dare-devil masculinity and BE A GIRL. And so strange are the almost irrelevant forebodings that invade one's consciousness in certain circumstances, I imagined and dreaded the embarrassing consequences should any stray German soldier take a fancy to my feminine charms and get fresh with me. I had heard of many both voluntary and enforced goings on in the occupied territories; affairs which would have cut to size our modern so-called *permissiveness* to the equivalent of an old spinsters' game of Patience ...

I was brought down to earth by her father, who suddenly reared from his tongue-tied state of utter incredulity. He furiously stressed his disapproval and denunciation of his daughter's declared intentions. Of all the maniacal notions to which he ever had to listen, he said, this was the most lunatic of all.

"You would be picked up by the Germans before you could even get out of Enghien," he maintained. All the German occupation troops in the town knew Madeleine (I could readily believe that) he argued, if only because she gave them the cold shoulder. Madeleine would assuredly meet the end that had befallen Nurse Cavell and, in addition, Mamma and he would be automatically implicated, with equally sinister results. Dad also made it very clear that he was quite unconcerned about my future, either for good or ill. His only worries were for his wife and daughter. As for me, I should be ashamed of myself for bringing such awful trouble on innocent people.

Throughout this row, Madeleine interjected fiery counter arguments, laced with family personalities which caused Mamma to weep and Father to rage. Eventually Father turned on me and me alone in an earnest and pleading way which I felt was meant to be a personal issue between just us two men. My command of the French language was not nearly equal to a proper understanding of some of the arguments, which were further complicated by a provincial accent. I could only grasp the trend of some of the goings on when Madeleine, with much reluctance, would occasionally interpret for my benefit.

Turning directly to me, father said:

"If you are a decent type and have any care at all for what is right, you will not expose my daughter to this terrible risk." Mamma shrieked.

"Nonsense!" yelled Madeleine.

At this my self respect made me reply with some vigour that I

107

had not known of Madeleine's plan to involve herself, and in any case I would make my escape alone and certainly without her. Here both Mamma and Madeleine became vociferous and earnestly entreated me to do no such thing. Any attempt on my part to get clear of the immediate district would be suicidal, they declared, without planned and expert help. Father then threw his trump card. He solemnly promised that if I would quietly *return to the prison* that same night he was sure he could arrange with an Escape Group to make a proper job of my get-away.

To me, however, the suggestion that I went back to the camp seemed preposterous and just the limit in nonsense. It struck me as the most crazy action thinkable, and I made known by wild word and gesture that my answer was an emphatic NO. At this, Papa's nerves really gave up the ghost and real terror took over. For some reason, or probably the lack of it, he began furtively opening and closing the door giving out onto the garden adjoining the prison. Every time he did this a shaft of light stabbed the vicinity patrolled by the camp sentries. Fortunately they took no notice of it, but it could have quickly led to trouble and I appealed to Papa, quite unsuccessfully, to calm down for a while.

His panic finally began to tell on me. It made me decide that, in the weird circumstances, my most sensible action after all would be to re-enter the camp, if I could possibly do so without detection, and await the properly planned escape that Father had promised. The alternative seemed quick disaster.

But how could I safely get back? I asked Father. It was a hazardous affair getting out – and that was indeed putting it mildly. Was it not almost a physical impossibility to scale the wall and re-enter, especially with the guards around?

When he realized that I was having nothing to do with Madelein's plan, Papa began to recover his self possession and became reasonably coherent. He explained that the ground was sunken like a moat immediately under the window from which I had dropped, but that on the corner of the building the ground level rose to within 4 or 5 ft of the window. IF the sentry did not see me, and IF the window had been left unsecured, I might get back unscathed.

In the event, both these IF's matured in my favour. When eventually, after over an hour of grovelling to earth because of the sentries, my scratched and bruised body did lower (hurl is perhaps the apposite word) itself through the window, to drop rather heavily on a dozing and aggrieved Private Hollowbone. I remained inert on the floor for an appreciable time. I was dejectedly and ruefully wondering if there could possibly be just one single other misguided *kriegsgefangener* who had twice escaped and voluntarily re-entered his prison both times within the same fortnight.

The Old Frau made her routine contact with me the following morning and had a lot to say about not being able to find me the previous night. The simple reason for this, I replied, was that the loose and dysentric nature of the so-called food in the prison these days was detaining some of us for long periods at the loo.

Madeleine very soon made contact with me again by means of a clandestine note, this time to let me know that there was a place in the fences and barricades surrounding the prison yard which tapered off to a gap narrow enough to allow conversation between us. If I would secrete myself there that same night, my lady friend would be on her side of this gap.

Although I now had reason to regard my lady's "plans" with some misgiving, I awaited nightfall with a gnawing impatience. Coupled with my eagerness to have something to do with her again, I was very anxious to warn her to be watchful of The Old Frau, who I was sure would be working on her suspicions of what I was up to.

So as soon as it was tolerably dark I was at the appointed location. There I found that by wriggling and squirming under some jagged hurdles, barbed wire and other obstacles, I ended up about 12ft from Madeleine. She had already managed to arrive nearby after similar manoeuvres on her side. The distance I have mentioned was the closest we could get to one another, but it was sufficiently near for us to exchange murmurs and sundry gestures – which grew ever more affectionate as the nights went by. Hardly the most aesthetic background to our romantic trysts, however, was the prison loo, the *urinoir* for which was one wall about 7ft high, placed transversely across the end of the prison yard and running almost at right angles from the precise spot where Madeleine and I exchanged our nightly cooings.

The loo was always in heavy and continuous use, more especially because of the sloppy and indigestible consistency of the camp diet. The result was a frequent series of explosive protests from abused stomachs which hardly enhanced the serene atmosphere pervading me and my lady friend. It says much for the powerful attraction of boy-girl relationships, however, that we mutely accepted the cacophony as the orchestra of a charmingly romantic affair.

*

Except for the daily working parties at Enghien railway station to load and unload German supplies and general goods of war, there was not now much hard labour for us. The men who had perpetrated their tricks of sabotage in the garages of Seclin and Roubaix were now deprived of that diversion. They had to be content with what inartistic opportunities for destruction came their way among the supplies they handled at Enghien railway station. It remains a most incredible thing in my memory that so much of this sabotage could go on without the Germans detecting it. How could they imagine the prisoners conscientiously applying themselves to anti-British acts without demur? Yet they apparently did. And so never a day went by without the prisoners damaging or displacing consignments they were put to load or unload. It really became too easy to do just that. So much so that one reckless party finally dropped something heavy through a crate of glass windscreens. The German guards simply could not avoid becoming aware of the crash and the presence of shattered glass. On the scene they promptly came. What had happened was too obvious for the miscreants to plead an accident; in fact, quite contrary to making any attempt to excuse themselves they stared out the German guards with defiant leers, gestures and even noises of the raspberry variety.

The Old Frau of course made all she could of this. She saw to it that I was personally pilloried for explanations by the German officer in charge of the local occupation troops. He made every effort to learn who among us actually did the damage, but we were now adept in drawing a misty veil over such acts. Eventually the officer curtly dismissed me from his sight with ravings about the punishments he intended to impose on the entire camp.

I shall never know what these reprisals were to be, because another advance by the Allied armies caused an order by the German Command the very next morning that the prisoners were to be cleared out of Enghien immediately. The vanguard of the advancing allied forces was still many miles distant, however, and it is probable that the Germans wanted any buildings, such as we prisoners occupied, for their retreating troops or military purposes.

Much as anything in the way of Allied victories, and especially their actual advances on the Western Front, was naturally an event of outstanding joy for us *kriegsgefangeners* my heart was heavy at the thought of being separated from Madeleine. I was but a boy with normal youthful reactions and I would have become attracted to her in any situation. The very unusual circumstances of our present liaison of course made the attachment all the more exciting.

We had reached the end of October 1918. Although we had no idea of the actual state of the war and the respective fortunes of the warring armies, we knew by many signs and portents that things were going very badly for our captors. We prisoners were moved off to Lembecque, a small scattered town on the main Tournai to Brussels road. Here we were interned in an improvised lock-up which was once a Tannery building. There remained only the signs that machinery was once in it. The Germans had long ago removed anything that looked like metal.

Other Allied prisoners of war were already in occupation, mainly Russians. There were also a few from the French Forces. We were all pitched into one lot together, regardless of nationality. This, in the primitive and barbarous conditions, did anything but advance the international amity which traditionally exists among Allies. Our fellows found the Russians particularly reticent, seemingly perverse, and disinclined to fraternise in the slightest way. Raids on the Russian food reserve (a carcass of horse-meat) by some Glaswegians (from the British lot) did nothing to ease any misunderstandings.

Although the German organization in general was obviously disintegrating, our gaolers maintained their tight watch on prisoners, and were all the more ruthless when dealing with escape attempts. For all that, there were a number of efforts to get away. I figured in one of them – and got no further than the Tannery exit. As the usual German sentries seemed less in evidence, the prospects seemed tempting. So one night I, with two others, had a go – and well, I will abbreviate a tale of ignominious failure by recording that my third "escape" was ended at the Tannery gate by the sudden appearance of a German captain yelling, "Where you go?" with his revolver in my belly.

Less fortunate even was one of the French soldier prisoners who tried his luck at the Freedom stakes. We had forced a window on the top floor of the Tannery building and were lowering the Frenchman to the ground, suspended by a length made up of all kinds of string, rope, wire and other materials which he had salved among debris in the Tannery and had knotted and tied together for his 35 ft descent. Half way down, the "rope" snapped, and our French friend plummetted to earth. Almost immediately afterwards we heard the inevitable German shouts and imprecations, followed shortly by some of them bursting into our apartment in their search for collaborators of the would-be escapee. By that time, however, we were all sprawled nonchalantly around, as guileless as kids at Sunday School. The Germans finally departed, cursing but clueless.

There were several dwelling houses in the vicinity of the Tannery at Lembecque, and it did not take the civilians long to make stealthy contact with the prisoners. These people were almost all women, whose men were with the Belgian or French armies, or had been removed to German labour camps, etc. Although, as I have said, the Germans kept their military prisoners on close rein, their ebbing fortunes of war at this time persuaded them to be a little less severe on the civil population. Where, not so many weeks previously, it might have been the firing squad for a civilian having anything to do with a prisoner, Belgian women were now openly making various friendly signs to us up at our windows.

We quickly developed a sign language which provided an adequate vehicle for mutual understanding. By this medium I was able even to learn from one amiable Belgian lady standing down in the road that she grew tobacco plants in her little garden. If I could let a string down one night she would tie on some leaves. So I did. And conceitedly crowing to myself that I had now got one over both the Germans and the Imperial Tobacco Company I carefully cut the leaves into minute strips and spread them over my patch of the floor to dry. This process seemed to take no end of time but the product eventually seemed burnable. I filled my pipe, the "tobacco" duly belched smoke, and with that inane gaze of bliss that they flog these days on television advertisements, I took about two deep puffs in and out – and passed out myself, or near enough. Either that Belgian lady had inadvertently got some exotic plant life mixed up with tobacco leaves or my health at that time was not man enough to stand smoking at all.

XVII

THE HARD WAY HOME

By early November 1918 we had become aware that something decisive was approaching with regard to the war. In captivity we could get no hard news at all. The Germans were as mute as oysters on the subject but we gathered from our bush telegraphy with the outside civilians that the Allies were advancing – and fast. Within a few days, and in obvious haste, the Germans bundled us out again, lined us up in marching order and moved us along the road to Brussels.

This main highway was in heavy use by the German transport, infantry and the other tools of war, and we prisoners were frequently halted for appreciable intervals to allow right of way to the more important members of the enemy machine. Several times our column was broken up and during one of these disarrays I, and one or two other prisoners, had to scuttle to the side of the road in order to let a hurrying staff car through. When our column reformed I remained where I was. Then some more transport came along, and in the renewed disorder the single German sentry (responsible for bringing along our rear) did not notice that I wasn't there.

For a few minutes I did not move, meanwhile trying to collect my senses and to decide what to do as I watched the column of prisoners slowly disappearing down the road. I recall having confused doubts that what I had done made any sense at all. However, I spotted an *estaminet*, the traditional Belgian cafe, a few hundred steps distant on the same side of the road. On the impulse I decided to enter this, with the idea of remaining inside there until dark, when I would take to the road when I had more coherently worked out some plans for getting myself clear of German-occupied territory. There seemed a fair chance of doing so now they were obviously retreating.

All seemed tranquil outside the *estaminet.* So I quickly walked in ... and found it chock full of German troops. Now at this date I was wearing an old dark overcoat, origin obscure. At any rate it belonged to no army that I knew of. I coveted it for its warmth, and it completely covered my old British army khaki tunic.

It was a *bistro* type *estaminet*, so I sauntered as calmly as I could to the bar. I had no idea what kind of drinks were current in Belgian pubs under German rule, but I took a chance and asked for a *Citron, s'il vous plait*. We used to buy citron and grenadine in the *estaminets* our side. The Belgian *patron* so far saw nothing odd about his new customer.

"*Voila Messieur,*" he said as he delivered my drink to the bar counter.

"*Combien, s'il vous plait?*" I asked: and precisely at that point it stood out a mile to our *patron* that he was now dealing with a customer who was a stranger and hadn't a clue as to what passed for money and how much of it in those parts and at that date.

"*Que voulez vous ...*" he began –

"*Je suis ...*" I interrupted, making a hush sign with my first finger over my lips. And to stop him blurting out any questions that would betray me to the Germans in the cafe (to whom I had my back turned as much as possible) I quietly unbuttoned the top of my old overcoat to expose my British army khaki tunic. Recognition was immediate, and on the instant our poor *patron* turned pale. Terror at what might happen to both of us (mainly to him, reasonably enough) was his concern if the Germans became aware that they had a wandering Tommy in their midst. Most Belgians justifiably dreaded the consequences of being mixed up with anything the Germans might suspect as collaborationist. There were many noble exceptions of course.

"*Il faut que je reste ici jusqu'a la nuit,*" I said quietly and slowly, praying that he would understand my plea in pidgin French to remain in his establishment until nightfall. He mutely wrestled for divine guidance in his unwelcome dilemma and that process took longer than was soothing to me during that interlude. But eventually he made furtive signs that I should follow him. He led me through his family living room and through his kitchen garden to a wooden structure which was soon to become too odorously familiar to me as the family lavatory.

"*Entrez ... and fermez la porte avec le ...*" Here the *patron* made a twisting sign with his fingers which meant that once inside I must fasten the door with the lock provided therein.

I did as I was told and as my eyes became accustomed to the gloom I found somewhere to sit, there to reflect, not very joyously, on my present predicament and uncertain future. The present was becoming intolerable. Those who remember the foul and putrid stench issuing from the primitive cesspool earthworks which passed for sanitation in many parts of continental Europe early this century will need no further description of my ordeal. I am sure that those who used these loos must have developed a mighty breath-and-nose-holding faculty which succoured them during the interval necessary for their visit.

I stuck this for about an hour and then ruefully concluded that there are some miseries worse than death. I fearfully crawled out of this stinking edifice and sought cover among some hen houses.

I decided to make for the British lines when and if I did move. In the ordinary way of static warfare, it would have been impossible to penetrate the various enemy trench systems and then cross No Man's Land to the British front trenches. Any sentry on the firestep would have shot to bits any such wayfarer before thinking of asking questions. There was no Halt Who Goes There? before pulling the trigger on things that moved in No Man's Land. But I reasoned it out that the Allied advance had ended the period of static trenches, at any rate for the time being. If the Germans were in fact retreating, their normal, efficient routine would be disorganized and, in the confusion, one unkempt bloke in an old, loose dark overcoat, trudging along in the opposite direction, would not be worth notice.

Since I had done my get-away on the spur of the moment, I had done none of the planning that was considered essential for these attempts. I had no food reserve of any kind. I did not have any kind of map, but my cyclist training had equipped me with a sketchy sense of the local topography. I knew that the road I was now actually on connected both German and Allied Armies, and if only I could remain on it all in one piece it would lead me straight through them. I also reckoned that the advance units of the British could be within 25 miles away. This can be a tremendous distance – and in my circumstances it actually *was* – but in the relative mental elixir of my new found freedom it seemed, well . . . not too far!

So with the coming of darkness I made a move westwards along the main Brussels – Tournai road, a highway that from the dawn of European habitation has been associated with historic and dramatic movements. It remains an important artery and is known to modern motorists as Road E 10 and the Belgian E 7. The road was a traditional tree-lined highway common to Flanders and France. Although I cautiously shambled along the verges and ditchsides there was, so far, no need for so much vigilance because I saw no living thing for the first few kilo-metres. But the sky was enflamed with several fitful conflagra-tions to the West.

Passing through the town of Halle, however, I had to cast one eye over my shoulder too often for comfort. Here, though it was well into the night, the Germans were active in the streets. Motorcyclists, staff cars and military transport seemed every-where, accompanied by much shouting, hooting and vehicular noise. I saw no civilians. They, I assumed, were strictly under curfew, especially in view of the turn of events. I am sure that all that saved me from being challenged and picked up was the darkness and the complete absence of artificial light providen-tially (for me) imposed by the frequent marauding bombers of the Royal Flying Corps.

For the next few hours I had to run (or rather crawl) the gauntlet of the numerous roadside service installations and habitations established by the Germans during four years of occupation. Incessant explosions were now taking place. These, I knew later, were German ammunition dumps being destroyed before they fell into Allied hands. Detonating missiles of all kinds and calibres added to the hullabaloo and general com-motion as they whistled and whined across the roadway in all directions. The highway became jammed several times with a snarl-up of German troops, gun carriages, horse and motor transport of all kinds; all struggling to extricate themselves from the confusion which comprised ditches, collisions, explo-sions and other unexpected obstructions. To move eastward was the dominant goal. Horses reared in fright at the explosions going on, while their German drivers cursed and yelled.

My progress in the opposite direction was accordingly stop-go, a matter of fits and starts. Many a time I had to lie low for an hour or so until the future seemed clear for a further tor-tuous half a mile. As the night wore on towards the dawn I noticed that the German military traffic was thinning out, but I arrived at one crossroad where there was extraordinary activity. Arrivals were halted and appeared to be receiving directions. Here I decided that it would be prudent for me to find a hide-out, if I could, until the following nightfall. In any case I felt worn out, and was in a bad way with hunger and thirst. I stumbled into a thicket nearby . . . and fell asleep for a couple of hours. Daylight and a November frost woke me. I fearfully looked around, but saw no sign of a single German or indeed any other form of life.

The sketchy itinery I had in mind when I quitted the *esta-*

minet envisaged my moving through the night and to lie up and hide under cover during daylight. In the ordinary way no escapee could of course remain long at large in the war area by daytime without being picked up. So I languished in my present hide-out while the morning dragged on ... with the extreme need of sustenance gnawing at my entrails. And hunger and thirst finally sapped my caution and it was not long after midday when I could stand it no longer. I had hoped that a chance civilian would stray my way, but life of any sort seemed to have fled the area. In fact the quietness was uncanny. Ironically enough, the silence made me more apprehensive and ill at ease than the explosions, crashes and noises of movement that were raging when I fell asleep.

Furtively I regained the highway and made along it for a good mile without seeing anyone. Then along the road in the distance I saw a house, probably a farm cottage. It would be, I feared, now used as a billet for German soldiers, in the same way as nearly every standing structure was used on the British side. For all that, I decided I must risk it and trust to luck that it was occupied by civilians who would give me a bite if it was only a raw potato – a humble eatable which on countless occasions has kept the wolf from the door for prisoners.

The house ran cheek by jowl with the road – no front garden, as is common in that part of Europe – and I tapped on the front door. An upstair window opened and, to my relief, a woman appeared.

"*Que voulez vous?*" or something like it, she asked, with an intonation quite devoid of joy at the prospect of meeting a stranger.

"*Puis je entrez pour un moment chez vous?*" I pleaded. "*Et alors je vous expliquez.*"

"*Etes vous Allemand?*" she demanded.

"*Non, non*" I replied. "*Je suis un soldat Anglais qui est prisonnier.*"

There was a pause.

"*Vous n'est pas un prisonnier encore,*" she then answered. "*La guerre est fini! L'Allemand tout parti.*"

And from that window I gathered from excited question and answer that the armistice had been declared that very morning. November 11, 1918!

The good lady then allowed me to enter her house. She gave me all she could spare from her very meagre store of food. This included a turnip and, what to me was a potential banquet, a real tomato. She also gave me a small piece of bread. If she ever received half the material benefits I prayed would reward her, her remaining days on earth were one carnival of riches.

I trudged along the road again, now in a trance. The news simply dazed me. I really could not come to sudden grips with a state of affairs where I was no longer in the clutches of a wretched captivity; that I was no longer a hunted creature; that I was now a human body which was not in imminent danger of erasure by explosives, asphyxiation by poison gas or dismemberment by sword or bayonet.

For a long time I saw no other person on my way – neither man nor beast. There were no noises save the belated explosions of distant ammunition dumps and depots which the Germans had time-fused just before their retreat. I was now in a military No-Man's-Land quite 40 miles wide, and those civilians who might be domiciled inside that bend were evidently remaining fast indoors until they were certain of the yet incredible fact that their oppressors had indeed finally departed. In any case the particular area I am describing was always sparsely populated.

I had vaguely reckoned on meeting up with the advance British somewhere between Ath and Tournai and although, in my real ignorance of anything like the actual situation, my "calculations" could only be based on some knowledge of the Belgian and French road systems, a measure of instinct and a lot of luck; and events were to prove that I was not far out.

My road back was through Enghien. Had the armistice not arrived and had I still been a prisoner on the run, I would not have dreamt of trying to contact Madeleine. That would of course have brought fearful risks to her and her family. But now, reasoned I with delight as I shambled along, everything was different. With my mind buoyed with the prospect of being with Madeleine again, I withstood the growing urge to subside for a while by the wayside. I was now sore, starving, thirsty, tired out and just about approaching the limit of all I could take.

Very late that night I literally staggered into Enghien. As I approached the town I picked up the sounds of revelry, although it must have been past midnight. Flags of the Allies bedecked every window and the narrow streets were choc-a-bloc with the milling inhabitants who, with linked arms, danced and sang to the accompaniment of every conceivable instrument which could issue music.

There was no doubt that the sudden end to the war found two broad differences in expression by those involved. The civilians, especially those in the zones that had been enemy occupied, justifiably gave vent to their relief in almost unrestrained gaiety. On the other hand, the fighting soldiers, who were every bit as relieved and thankful (probably more so) at the cessation of the holocausts, found expression for their profound feelings in a quieter, more subdued and thoughtful survey of the past and present events that had befallen them individually. There were exceptions, but I am sure this was the general picture.

I was tolerably certain that Madeleine and probably her father and mother would be out of doors among the festive locals. In that case I would simply huddle down in their doorway and sleep until they returned. But, as I tapped on the front door, which gave out immediately on to the street, it was opened almost at once – by Madeleine. The reception I received is a memory that soars higher than I can describe with adequate words. Her parents were very demonstrative with their sincere welcome, particularly Papa who was anxious to remove from my mind any suspicion that he still harboured the hostility he had (reasonably) betrayed towards me on the night I escaped from the prison.

"But Willy! Your face has gone," exclaimed Madeleine, compressing her own cheeks with her thumb and first finger to signify my protruding cheek bones. Mamma providentially divined this as evidence that I had gone grievously short of sustenance. Whereupon she and Madeleine raked out what there was in the house in the way of something to eat ... and I did what I could to show some semblance of table manners, a control which imposed no little strain on me in my famished state. Some family friends looked in, even though it had gone midnight. Papa unearthed some wine, which had been put away for "the day". I had one glass of it. A stimulant at first, it very soon had the opposite effect on my exhausted self, and I actually fell asleep during the party. Papa roused me to insert my somnolent body in a suit of his pyjamas. He piloted me to a bed on which I sank into one of those sleeps that overtake us mortals seldom in a lifetime. It was my first ordinary bed for over two years (when I had ten days' leave in England). I was between clean, white bedsheets, wearing real pyjamas, and in a room to myself. And there was no war.

As my confused impressions gradually resumed rational shape, in the way they do after deep sleep, I became slowly aware of some aspects on the seamy side of the outlook. Here was I in bed linen and sleeping ware which screamed with purity and whiteness, and I was as lousy as the proverbial coot with a body that had not been bathed for months. The enormity of this unwholesome combination levered me out of the bed and I resolved to explain to Papa my shame and earnest wish for some remedial action. Which I did.

I lingered for two extremely happy days at Enghien, during which my mutual attachment with Madeleine blossomed to the extent that Papa quite bluntly imposed a bar to our being quite alone anywhere. Madeleine *promenaded* with me in Enghien's streets. She was obviously the belle of the town and very popular with everyone. We visited together many of her friends. I was now the only English soldier they had in the district and I was feted out of all proportion to my importance or my deserts. However, it made me try to be a bit more presentable by tidying up my old uniform as much as I could, and polishing my brass buttons and cap badge etc. – every single item of which I soon lost to the local girls for souvenirs.

November 14, three days after the Armistice, and there was still no sign of any advance patrol from the British front, although someone did report that a lone British cavalry reconnaissance trooper had entered Ath the previous day, a place about 12 miles Westward. He was hanging over his horse, paralytic drunk. The people everywhere had ran out to greet him with glasses of wine!

Very much refreshed I naturally became rather impatient to regain our lines and see England again. I pushed on once more. The one emotional snag was parting from Madeleine and for me it was a tremendous wrench. We had formed a sincere and delightful attachment, as the future was to prove, but she readily appreciated my eagerness to rejoin my mother and life at home, as soon as possible after all these vicissitudes.

The road from Enghien to Ath was now thronged with civilian men, women, children and animals pushing every conceivable contraption on wheels that would move goods. Those not owning such transport plodded along with parcels and bundles tied all around them. They were evacuees in reverse. In other words they were civilians returning to their former habitats (if they were still standing) from which they had been driven by the Germans or military action during the four years of war. It was a human journey which oozed pathos. Before I reached Ath I had helped several old ladies along on their way with at least one of their bundles.

Entering Ath, I met the first contingent which officially represented any of the Allied forces, and it was an Italian Army service unit. It surprised me that Italian soldiers should form our vanguard. Anyway, they treated me royally. I was the first returning prisoner they had come across and they were all very curious to know what I could tell them about life beyond the barrier. They took me to their temporary headquarters in Ath and gave me a huge meal of meat and vegetables from the good and generous rations that were the normal issue for the British army all through the war ... I shall never forget this, my first good square meal since I was taken prisoner, and I shall never forget the abdominal aftermath about two hours later. I learnt that the change to good diet had the same dysentric effect as had the change to the prisoner diet. The stomach does not accept such sudden alterations.

The Italians told me that the nearest advance British troops at that moment were in Tournai, about 20 miles further on. They had kindly established this news for me by their field telephones. They would not hear of my attempting the remainder of the journey on foot. If I would wait a little they would arrange something to take me there. The *something* turned out to be a large size in motor trucks.

Half way to Tournai, the Italian driver spotted a British staff car sporting a Union Jack on the radiator. It was an official British war correspondent, who took my story and also several photographs of me. One of these later found a place in the Imperial War Museum because it portrayed the first British prisoner to regain the Allied lines over that particular sector. The picture remains in the Museum.

My Italian friends duly delivered me to British Headquarters at Tournai. Here I was treated with almost passionate care, an emotive experience which can be fully appreciated only by those who have returned to British hands after enforced exile. I was bathed, fed, bedded and reclothed. After several days other prisoners began to crawl in, almost all of them in a condition far more wretched than mine because they had not had the benefit of the halfway "convalescence" I had enjoyed at Enghien.

Most of the prisoners told the same harrowing story. Soon after the news of the Armistice, the Germans simply scurried off in haste away from possible Allied reach. They abandoned their prisoners, exposed and foodless, to make the best of it. Although scores of prisoners never made it, and finished by the roadsides, I really do not quite know how the Germans could have managed otherwise. The Germans were the target of no end of furious and revengeful threats from the Allied side because of the prisoners' plight, but some cool assessment of the circumstances might not be out of place. On the morning of November 11 1918 the German troops in many parts of France and Flanders were in headlong retreat. Isolated Germans such as those guarding prison camps were suddenly fearful of their captives' reaction and the civilians' "night of the long knives". It is remarkable that neither matured to any significant extent. Moreover, the coming of the Armistice was the unofficial signal for all British prisoners held in France and Belgium to make a bolt towards the West, and no Germans could have persuaded them to go the other way, even by limousines.

After six days of care and any advisable medical treatment at Tournai, during which some 50 other prisoners had gathered, a specially laid on Red Cross train took us to Calais from where a Red Cross steamer took us to Dover. Those prisoners well enough to stand on deck watched the approaching white cliffs in passionate and awed silence. When the boat actually entered the harbour the sirens of the assembled ships, railway engine whistles and anything that could make noise gave us a cacophonous welcome – and an emotional experience. This was the very first boat bringing home-coming prisoners of war. None of us reacted to this wonderful reception with any outward sign of joy. None of us even waved. Our feelings were too pregnant for any banalities. Years later I saw television pictures of repatriated American prisoners from Korea kissing the earth on landing. I understood why.

All prisoners, or all those with normal reactions, suffer a sense of humiliation for having been captured and, if only for that reason we did not look for or expect any tumultous reception on our return home. When on the contrary this did happen it was so totally unexpected that while it invoked in us an overwhelming sense of relief and gratitude it benumbed us when it first hit us. The sympathy shown to returned prisoners in Britain took extraordinary turns. My Army Discharge Certificate bears the following entries in the space reserved for Military Qualifications: 1. Artificer 2. Machine Gunner: 3. *Prisoner-of-War* (my italics) I know of no other Army which regards capture by the enemy as a Military *Qualification*. Were it not of course that the intention was compassionate, the connection could exist only in comic opera.

Food rationing for meat and some other victuals was in force in Britain at the end of the war and everyone had ration cards. But boldly written in ink at the top of the food cards issued to us repatriates were the words REPATRIATED PRISONER OF WAR. Although that did not nominally exempt us from the rationing rules, no waitress would ever accept such food coupons tendered by an ex-prisoner on receiving his meal.

At Dover we were housed for the night in a commandeered hotel close by the famous Castle, and in the morning some army doctors medically inspected us for fear of our taking any diseases home. In their sincere desire not to put any avoidable obstructions in the way of our speedy return, these worthy doctors made the most cursory examination imaginable. Within a few hours we were luxuriously esconsed in a train, again a Red Cross conveyance, which terminated at Cannon Street station in London.

Almost the first person to spot me leaving the carriage was my elder brother. By virtue of holding a job at the War Office he had access to knowledge of the arrival of the very first train expected to arrive in London with returned prisoners. He had not the slightest information of what had happened to me or where I had been since capture, and he waited at Cannon Street station if only to glean some chance news from those leaving the train. And to his extreme astonishment, I came face to face with him.

At the platform exit barriers there were gathered some groups of well-intentioned ladies whose key-job friends must also have tipped them off about a train carrying repatriated prisoners. As I left the exit with my brother – there were no other prisoners with me – all these ladies clapped and chanted "bravo". This manifestation was undoubtedly well meant and very sincere, but I must confess I felt miserably self-conscious and embarrassed.

The traffic policeman in Cannon Street outside the railway station added his contribution to our welcome by immediately and ostentatiously halting the traffic while I crossed the road, as my fascinated gaze absorbed the London scene with which I, as one of its citizens, had once been so familiar.

On the way from Cannon Street to my home in North London the taxi driver was sufficiently interested in his uniformed passenger to elicit from my brother that I was an ex-prisoner just repatriated from the Germans. The driver refused to accept any fare at the end of the journey.

An obviously care-worn and ageing lady quietly opened the door in response to our knock. She, my mother, had no idea where I might have been at that moment, if and when I would be coming home at all, or even if I was still alive. Her eyes seemed to absorb me for a long time, with not a word. She then impulsively enfolded me in that kind of embrace which can emanate only from a mother who has been officially informed that her son had been killed.

POSTSCRIPT

Had this been a novel there would reasonably have been an appropriate climax of wedding bells with Madeleine as the romantic heroine, but as these memoirs are based on facts there must be no fictional conclusion.

Although our mutual attraction was very real and any future short of an everlasting alliance was unthinkable, marriage was never at any time mentioned by either of us. In the less excitable circumstances of post-war, it gradually became apparent that several artificial shadows loomed over the prospects of an inter-continental betrothal leading to prolonged marital bliss in our cases.

I wed an English girl, Dorothy, the sister of one of my army friends who was taken prisoner with me. My marriage to her was the finest thing that has ever favoured me. Whether the same could be said for her is open to grave doubt. However, for over 50 years I have received the affection and care of a woman and mother dedicated to loyalty and high principle which at times has put my comparatively ignoble conduct to shame.

Her brother, alas, died some time after repatriation with disabilities aggravated by privations during captivity.

As for Madeleine, our friendship flowered into one of those exquisite, dedicated and life-long affairs which, as a rule, can only remain permanently so when unblunted by physical marriage. We kept in continuous touch. She and my wife became close friends. We met in Brussels or England two or three times annually for nearly 50 years until Madeleine died in Liége in 1967 – since when Belgium ceased to be the same for me.

Teresa, my courageous young lady of Roubaix, reached England soon after the Armistice. My brother's address, which I had managed to slip to her in the prison Commandant's office, was the means of our reunion. We had much to do with each other thereafter, and some of these meetings developed into such tempestuous affairs as might be expected from a lady of her spirit when she could not get her own way. She is now enjoying a happy second marriage, lives in New Zealand, and we regularly exchange letters to this day, 54 years after our first meeting as prisoners.

As was predictable, my war service had a profound effect upon my estimates of life's true values and caused some drastic changes in my accepted dogmas. True I had every reason to be thankful for having emerged comparatively unscathed, but the dreadful sufferings I had seen resigned me to the unspiritual conclusion that mankind is also governed by the "Nature red in tooth and claw" law.

But I'm very glad I didn't miss it.

NEL BESTSELLERS

Crime

T013	332	CLOUDS OF WITNESS	*Dorothy L. Sayers* 40p
T016	307	THE UNPLEASANTNESS AT THE BELLONA CLUB	*Dorothy L. Sayers* 40p
T021	548	GAUDY NIGHT	*Dorothy L. Sayers* 40p
T026	698	THE NINE TAILORS	*Dorothy L. Sayers* 50p
T026	671	FIVE RED HERRINGS	*Dorothy L. Sayers* 50p
T015	556	MURDER MUST ADVERTISE	*Dorothy L. Sayers* 40p

Fiction

T018	520	HATTER'S CASTLE	*A. J. Cronin* 75p
T013	944	CRUSADER'S TOMB	*A. J. Cronin* 60p
T013	936	THE JUDAS TREE	*A. J. Cronin* 50p
T015	386	THE NORTHERN LIGHT	*A. J. Cronin* 50p
T026	213	THE CITADEL	*A. J. Cronin* 80p
T027	112	BEYOND THIS PLACE	*A. J. Cronin* 60p
T016	609	KEYS OF THE KINGDOM	*A. J. Cronin* 50p
T027	201	THE STARS LOOK DOWN	*A. J. Cronin* 90p
T018	539	A SONG OF SIXPENCE	*A. J. Cronin* 50p
T001	288	THE TROUBLE WITH LAZY ETHEL	*Ernest K. Gann* 30p
T003	922	IN THE COMPANY OF EAGLES	*Ernest K. Gann* 30p
T023	001	WILDERNESS BOY	*Stephen Harper* 35p
T017	524	MAGGIE D	*Adam Kennedy* 60p
T022	390	A HERO OF OUR TIME	*Mikhail Lermontov* 45p
T025	691	SIR, YOU BASTARD	*G. F. Newman* 40p
T022	536	THE HARRAD EXPERIMENT	*Robert H. Rimmer* 50p
T022	994	THE DREAM MERCHANTS	*Harold Robbins* 95p
T023	303	THE PIRATE	*Harold Robbins* 95p
T022	968	THE CARPETBAGGERS	*Harold Robbins* £1.00
T016	560	WHERE LOVE HAS GONE	*Harold Robbins* 75p
T023	958	THE ADVENTURERS	*Harold Robbins* £1.00
T025	241	THE INHERITORS	*Harold Robbins* 90p
T025	276	STILETTO	*Harold Robbins* 50p
T025	268	NEVER LEAVE ME	*Harold Robbins* 50p
T025	292	NEVER LOVE A STRANGER	*Harold Robbins* 90p
T022	226	A STONE FOR DANNY FISHER	*Harold Robbins* 80p
T025	284	79 PARK AVENUE	*Harold Robbins* 75p
T025	187	THE BETSY	*Harold Robbins* 80p
T020	894	RICH MAN, POOR MAN	*Irwin Shaw* 90p

Historical

T022	196	KNIGHT WITH ARMOUR	*Alfred Duggan* 50p
T022	250	THE LADY FOR RANSOM	*Alfred Duggan* 50p
T015	297	COUNT BOHEMOND	*Alfred Duggan* 50p
T017	958	FOUNDING FATHERS	*Alfred Duggan* 50p
T017	753	WINTER QUARTERS	*Alfred Duggan* 50p
T021	297	FAMILY FAVOURITES	*Alfred Duggan* 50p
T022	625	LEOPARDS AND LILIES	*Alfred Duggan* 60p
T019	624	THE LITTLE EMPERORS	*Alfred Duggan* 50p
T020	126	THREE'S COMPANY	*Alfred Duggan* 50p
T021	300	FOX 10: BOARDERS AWAY	*Adam Hardy* 35p

Science Fiction

T016	900	STRANGER IN A STRANGE LAND	*Robert Heinlein* 75p
T020	797	STAR BEAST	*Robert Heinlein* 35p
T017	451	I WILL FEAR NO EVIL	*Robert Heinlein* 80p
T026	817	THE HEAVEN MAKERS	*Frank Herbert* 35p
T027	279	DUNE	*Frank Herbert* 90p
T022	854	DUNE MESSIAH	*Frank Herbert* 60p
T023	974	THE GREEN BRAIN	*Frank Herbert* 35p
T012	859	QUEST FOR THE FUTURE	*A. E. Van Vogt* 35p
T015	270	THE WEAPON MAKERS	*A. E. Van Vogt* 30p
T023	265	EMPIRE OF THE ATOM	*A. E. Van Vogt* 40p
T017	354	THE FAR-OUT WORLDS OF A. E. VAN VOGT	*A. E. Van Vogt* 40p

NEL BESTSELLERS

War

T027	066	COLDITZ: THE GERMAN STORY	*Reinhold Eggers*	50p
T009	890	THE K BOATS	*Don Everett*	30p
T020	854	THE GOOD SHEPHERD	*C. S. Forester*	35p
T012	999	P.Q.17 – CONVOY TO HELL	*Lund & Ludlam*	30p
T026	299	TRAWLERS GO TO WAR	*Lund & Ludlam*	50p
T010	872	BLACK SATURDAY	*Alexander McKee*	30p
T020	495	ILLUSTRIOUS	*Kenneth Poolman*	40p
T018	032	ARK ROYAL	*Kenneth Poolman*	40p
T027	198	THE GREEN BERET	*Hilary St. George Saunders*	50p
T027	171	THE RED BERET	*Hilary St. George Saunders*	50p

Western

T016	994	EDGE NO. 1: THE LONER	*George Gilman*	30p
T024	040	EDGE NO. 2: TEN THOUSAND DOLLARS AMERICAN	*George Gilman*	35p
T024	075	EDGE NO. 3: APACHE DEATH	*George Gilman*	35p
T024	032	EDGE NO. 4: KILLER'S BREED	*George Gilman*	35p
T023	990	EDGE NO. 5: BLOOD ON SILVER	*George Gilman*	35p
T020	002	EDGE NO. 14: THE BIG GOLD	*George Gilman*	30p

General

T017	400	CHOPPER	*Peter Cave*	30p
T022	838	MAMA	*Peter Cave*	35p
T021	009	SEX MANNERS FOR MEN	*Robert Chartham*	35p
T019	403	SEX MANNERS FOR ADVANCED LOVERS	*Robert Chartham*	30p
T023	206	THE BOOK OF LOVE	*Dr. David Delvin*	90p
P002	368	AN ABZ OF LOVE	*Inge & Stan Hegeler*	75p
P011	402	A HAPPIER SEX LIFE	*Dr. Sha Kokken*	70p
W24	79	AN ODOUR OF SANCTITY	*Frank Yerby*	50p
W28	24	THE FOXES OF HARROW	*Frank Yerby*	50p

Mad

S006	086	MADVERTISING		40p
S006	292	MORE SNAPPY ANSWERS TO STUPID QUESTIONS		40p
S006	425	VOODOO MAD		40p
S006	293	MAD POWER		40p
S006	291	HOPPING MAD		40p

NEL P.O. BOX 11, FALMOUTH, CORNWALL

For U.K. and Eire: customers should include to cover postage, 15p for the first book plus 5p per copy for each additional book ordered, up to a maximum charge of 50p.

For Overseas customers and B.F.P.O.: customers should include to cover postage, 20p for the first book and 10p per copy for each additional book.

Name...

Address ....

....

Title ....
(May)